HOW TO FILE YOUR OWN BANKRUPTCY

(or How to Avoid It)

Fifth Edition

Edward A. Haman
Attorney at Law

SPHINX® PUBLISHING
AN IMPRINT OF SOURCEBOOKS, INC.®
NAPERVILLE, ILLINOIS
www.SphinxLegal.com

Copyright © 1990, 1992, 1994, 1998, and 2002 by Edward A. Haman

All rights reserved. No part of this book may be reproduced in any form or by any electronic or mechanical means including information storage and retrieval systems—except in the case of brief quotations embodied in critical articles or reviews—without permission in writing from its publisher, Sourcebooks, Inc.® Purchasers of the book are granted a license to use the forms contained herein for their own personal use. No claim of copyright is made in any official government forms reproduced herein.

Fifth Edition, 2002
Second Printing, January, 2003

Published by: **Sphinx® Publishing, An Imprint of Sourcebooks, Inc.®**

<u>Naperville Office</u>
P.O. Box 4410
Naperville, Illinois 60567-4410
630-961-3900
Fax: 630-961-2168
www.sourcebooks.com
www.SphinxLegal.com

This publication is designed to provide accurate and authoritative information in regard to the subject matter covered. It is sold with the understanding that the publisher is not engaged in rendering legal, accounting, or other professional service. If legal advice or other expert assistance is required, the services of a competent professional person should be sought.

From a Declaration of Principles Jointly Adopted by a Committee of the American Bar Association and a Committee of Publishers and Associations

This product is not a substitute for legal advice.

Disclaimer required by Texas statutes.

Library of Congress Cataloging-in-Publication Data
Haman, Edward A.
How to file your own bankruptcy (or how to avoid it) / Edward A. Haman.-- 5th ed.
p. cm. -- (Legal survival guides)
Includes index.
ISBN 1-57248-191-9
1. Bankruptcy--United States--Popular works. 2. Bankruptcy--United States--Forms. I. Title. II. Series.

KF1524.6 .H36 2001
346.7307'8--dc21

2001054288

Printed and bound in the United States of America.

VHG Paperback — 10 9 8 7 6 5 4 3 2

CONTENTS

Using Self-Help Law Books

Before using a self-help law book, you should realize the advantages and disadvantages of doing your own legal work and understand the challenges and diligence that this requires.

THE GROWING
TREND

Rest assured that you won't be the first or only person handling your own legal matter. For example, in some states, more than seventy-five percent of divorces and other cases have at least one party representing him or herself. Because of the high cost of legal services, this is a major trend and many courts are struggling to make it easier for people to represent themselves. However, some courts are not happy with people who do not use attorneys and refuse to help them in any way. For some, the attitude is, "Go to the law library and figure it out for yourself."

We at Sphinx write and publish self-help law books to give people an alternative to the often complicated and confusing legal books found in most law libraries. We have made the explanations of the law as simple and easy to understand as possible. Of course, unlike an attorney advising an individual client, we cannot cover every conceivable possibility.

COST/VALUE
ANALYSIS

Whenever you shop for a product or service, you are faced with various levels of quality and price. In deciding what product or service to buy, you make a cost/value analysis on the basis of your willingness to pay and the quality you desire.

When buying a car, you decide whether you want transportation, comfort, status, or sex appeal. Accordingly, you decide among such choices as a Neon, a Lincoln, a Rolls Royce, or a Porsche. Before making a decision, you usually weigh the merits of each option against the cost.

When you get a headache, you can take a pain reliever (such as aspirin) or visit a medical specialist for a neurological examination. Given this choice, most people, of course, take a pain reliever, since it costs only pennies; whereas a medical examination costs hundreds of dollars and takes a lot of time. This is usually a logical choice because it is rare to need anything more than a pain reliever for a headache. But in some cases, a headache may indicate a brain tumor and failing to see a specialist right away can result in complications. Should everyone with a headache go to a specialist? Of course not, but people treating their own illnesses must realize that they are betting on the basis of their cost/value analysis of the situation. They are taking the most logical option.

The same cost/value analysis must be made when deciding to do one's own legal work. Many legal situations are very straight forward, requiring a simple form and no complicated analysis. Anyone with a little intelligence and a book of instructions can handle the matter without outside help.

But there is always the chance that complications are involved that only an attorney would notice. To simplify the law into a book like this, several legal cases often must be condensed into a single sentence or paragraph. Otherwise, the book would be several hundred pages long and too complicated for most people. However, this simplification necessarily leaves out many details and nuances that would apply to special or unusual situations. Also, there are many ways to interpret most legal questions. Your case may come before a judge who disagrees with the analysis of our authors.

Therefore, in deciding to use a self-help law book and to do your own legal work, you must realize that you are making a cost/value analysis. You have decided that the money you will save in doing it yourself outweighs the chance that your case will not turn out to your satisfaction. Most people handling their own simple legal matters never have a problem, but occasionally people find that it ended up costing them more to have an attorney straighten out the situation than it would have if they had hired an attorney in the beginning. Keep this in mind if you decide to handle your own case, and be sure to consult an attorney if you feel you might need further guidance.

LOCAL RULES   The next thing to remember is that a book which covers the law for the entire nation, or even for an entire state, cannot possibly include every procedural difference of every county or federal district court. Whenever possible, we provide the exact form needed; however, in some areas, each county or federal district, or even each judge, may require unique forms and procedures. In our *state* books, our forms usually cover the majority of counties in the state, or provide examples of the type of form that will be required. In our *national* books, our forms are sometimes even more general in nature but are designed to give a good idea of the type of form that will be needed in most locations. Nonetheless, keep in mind that your *state*, county, federal district, or judge may have a requirement, or use a form, that is not included in this book.

You should not necessarily expect to be able to get all of the information and resources you need solely from within the pages of this book. This book will serve as your guide, giving you specific information whenever possible and helping you to find out what else you will need to know. This is just like if you decided to build your own backyard deck. You might purchase a book on how to build decks. However, such a book would not include the building codes and permit requirements of every city, town, county, and township in the nation; nor would it include the lumber, nails, saws, hammers, and other materials and tools you would need to actually build the deck. You would use the book as your guide, and then do some work and research involving such matters as whether you need a permit of some kind, what type and grade of wood are available in your area, whether to use hand tools or power tools, and how to use those tools.

Before using the forms in a book like this, you should check with your court clerk to see if there are any local rules of which you should be aware, or local forms you will need to use. Often, such forms will require the same information as the forms in the book but are merely laid out differently, use slightly different language, or use different color paper so the clerks can easily find them. They will sometimes require additional information.

CHANGES IN THE LAW

Besides being subject to state and local rules and practices, the law is subject to change at any time. The courts and the legislatures of all fifty states are constantly revising the laws. It is possible that while you are reading this book, some aspect of the law is being changed or that a court is interpreting a law in a different way. You should always check the most recent statutes, rules and regulations to see what, if any changes have been made.

In most cases, the change will be of minimal significance. A form will be redesigned, additional information will be required, or a waiting period will be extended. As a result, you might need to revise a form, file an extra form, or wait out a longer time period; these types of changes will not usually affect the outcome of your case. On the other hand, sometimes a major part of the law is changed, the entire law in a particular area is rewritten, or a case that was the basis of a central legal point is overruled. In such instances, your entire ability to pursue your case may be impaired.

To help you with local requirements and changes in the law, be sure to read Section 5, page 46 on "Legal Research."

Again, you should weigh the value of your case against the cost of an attorney and make a decision as to what you believe is in your best interest.

INTRODUCTION

Is this book for you? You are probably feeling burdened by your financial situation, or else you wouldn't be reading this. If you are like most Americans, you are probably struggling to make payments on a mortgage, car loan, medical bills, various credit cards, and possibly a student loan, home improvement loan, or other consumer debts. Perhaps you have been laid-off at work due to a generally slowing economy, or due to problems with your company or industry. Maybe you, or a member of your family, has had a serious illness or injury, and many of the medical bills were not covered by insurance.

This book is designed specifically for you. It will help you analyze your situation, decide whether you should file for bankruptcy, and guide you through the steps to either avoid bankruptcy or get through the bankruptcy procedure. This is not a law school course, but a practical guide to get you through "the system" as easily as possible.

This book presents fairly simplified procedures for use by non-attorneys. It does not contain all the possible loopholes or tricks of the trade that an experienced bankruptcy lawyer might use to gain a little extra advantage. On the other hand, for many people, these legal details either don't apply, or their advantage will be offset by not having to pay the fee of an experienced bankruptcy attorney.

If you are at a high income level, or have extensive and complicated investments and debts, you will need a lawyer. However, this book will still help you to understand the system and work with your lawyer more effectively. **Note:** *This book is not designed for corporate, partnership, or business-related bankruptcies.*

Bankruptcy law is covered in various chapters of the federal Bankruptcy Code. This book covers bankruptcy under Chapter 7 and Chapter 13 of the Bankruptcy Code. In order to avoid confusion between chapters of the Bankruptcy Code and what would normally be called chapters of this book, the word section will be used instead of the word chapter when referring to this book. The word chapter will only be used when referring to the Bankruptcy Code.

Sections 1 through 5 of this book will explain the legal system, help you decide if bankruptcy is for you, and help you prepare for filing for bankruptcy. Section 6 will explain what forms you need and how to prepare them. Section 7 explains the bankruptcy court procedures. Section 8 deals with special circumstances that may arise, and Section 9 gives you some advice for the future once you have completed your bankruptcy case in court.

Appendix A contains the federal and state lists of property that you may keep even if you file for bankruptcy, and Appendix B provides some checklists for filing bankruptcy. Appendix C provides worksheets that will help you fill in the forms in Appendix D. If you have to write to creditors, Appendix E has some sample letters.

Be sure to read this entire book, especially Section 6 on "Understanding Legal Forms," before you begin preparing any of the forms in this book. You may want to make several copies of the forms in this book, and save the originals in order to make more copies if you need them.

NOTE: *For some time, Congress has been discussing important changes to the bankruptcy law. The changes being considered include limiting the amount of the homestead exemption, creating financial criteria for filing for bankruptcy, and requiring credit counseling before filing.*

At the time of the Second Printing, Congress had not yet passed any changes to bankruptcy legislation.

BANKRUPTCY AND THE LEGAL SYSTEM

1

Simply stated, *bankruptcy* is a legal procedure that allows you to get out of oppressive debt, and get a fresh start financially. The concept of bankruptcy goes back at least to the time of the Old Testament, where it states: "At the end of every seven years you shall grant a release and this is the manner of the release: every creditor shall release what he has lent to his neighbor…" (Deuteronomy 15:1-2).

HISTORY AND GENERAL INFORMATION

In the United States, the importance of bankruptcy was recognized at the time of our nation's birth, and was made a part of the U.S. Constitution. Article I, Section 8 of the U.S. Constitution gives Congress the power to establish "uniform laws on the subject of bankruptcies throughout the United States." In 1800, Congress enacted the first bankruptcy laws.

Today, there exists a comprehensive set of federal laws that govern bankruptcy. There are so many bankruptcies filed each year that there is a special division of the federal court system devoted exclusively to bankruptcy. In recent years, bankruptcy filings have reached over one-million annually. So if you need to file for bankruptcy, you can be sure you will not be alone.

PURPOSE AND PROCEDURE

The bankruptcy procedure serves two purposes. First, it allows you to change your financial situation. Second, it holds your creditors at bay while you make this change.

You also have a choice about changing your situation. You can choose either of two procedures. The first is *traditional bankruptcy*, where your debts are forgiven altogether. The other procedure is referred to as a *re-organization*, *wage-earner plan*, or *payment plan*. In this procedure, you arrange to pay off some or all of your debts according to a payment plan that you can handle on your income. Although this is technically not bankruptcy, it is a part of the bankruptcy law and will be referred to in this book as a bankruptcy.

CHAPTERS OF
BANKRUPTCY

Traditional bankruptcy is covered in Chapter 7 of the federal Bankruptcy Code, and is often referred to as a *Chapter 7*. The payment plan procedure is covered in Chapter 13 of the Bankruptcy Code, and is referred to as a *Chapter 13*. These procedures will be discussed in greater detail in later sections of this book. (When referring to parts of this book, the word *section* will be used instead of the word *chapter*, to help avoid confusion with chapters of the Bankruptcy Code.)

There are other chapters to the Bankruptcy Code. *Chapter 12* is specially designed for farmers, so if you are a farmer you should consult a bankruptcy lawyer. *Chapter 11* is generally designed for corporations and partnerships. Chapter 11 is also available to individuals, although it is not used unless the person has secured debts in excess of $350,000, unsecured debts in excess of $100,000, and sufficient income to pay off a portion of these debts over several years. If you are in this situation you should consult a lawyer.

THE LEGAL SYSTEM

This section will give you a general introduction to the legal system of the bankruptcy court. Most people have an idea of the way the legal system *should* be, which usually does not match the realities of the system. If you don't learn to accept the realities, you will experience much stress and frustration. Although bankruptcy can get as complicated as any other area of law, for most cases it is a bit more cut and dried and predictable than many other areas.

RULES   Our legal system is a system of rules. There are basically three types of rules:

1. *Rules of Law*: These provide the basic substance of the law, such as defining a debt and describing what property can be kept after bankruptcy.

2. *Rules of Procedure*: These outline how matters are to be handled in the courts, such as requiring court papers to be in a certain form, or filed within a certain time.

3. *Rules of Evidence*: These set forth the manner in which facts are to be proven.

In bankruptcy it is not usually necessary to be concerned with rules of evidence. Most bankruptcy cases are presented to the court in the way of standard forms. It is unnecessary to call witnesses and introduce evidence as would be done in a trial of another type of case. In addition, the rules of law and procedure are so well defined that, in most cases, they are not nearly as complicated and subject to interpretation as in many other areas. For most middle-class Americans, bankruptcy is mostly filling out certain forms, filing them with the court, and attending a couple of meetings. As long as you provide the court with accurate and complete information about your finances, you shouldn't have any difficulties.

A basic rule of this book is *don't panic!* If, as you read, you find yourself thinking "I'll never be able to do this myself," *keep reading*. By the end of this book, you'll see that it is a fairly simple task.

The advice "don't panic" also applies to dealing with the court. The United States is divided into numerous districts, and each district has its own bankruptcy court. Each court has a court clerk, and may have some local rules. It is possible that the clerk in your district will tell you that one of your papers is not exactly correct in its form or content. This happens to lawyers with many years of experience, so there is no need to feel bad if it happens to you. If this happens to you, all you can do is relax, find out exactly what the clerk wants, and do it the clerk's way. Similar to the old saying about the army, there is the right way, the wrong way, and the clerk's way. Only the clerk's way will get you what you want. Fortunately, the forms are standardized all over the country, so this should not be a problem.

THE SYSTEM

Although bankruptcy is relatively simple and straight-forward, there are a few realities of our nation's legal system that can apply to all areas of the law to some degree. A brief mention of these realities may prepare you in the event you come across any of them.

The system is not perfect. The rules are designed to apply to all persons in all situations. This can sometimes lead to an unfair result if one person's situation is slightly different.

It is also possible for a judge to make a bad call, or for someone to cheat and not get caught (such as by not telling the truth even under oath). As a well-known and respected judge once said to the young attorney: "This is a court of law, young man, not a court of justice!"

Judges don't always follow the rules. This is a shocking discovery for many young lawyers. After spending three years in law school learning legal theory, and after spending countless hours preparing for a hearing in which all of the law is on your side, you find that the judge isn't going to pay any attention to legal theories and the law. As one judge is known to have put it: "In my courtroom, the law is what I say it is."

Many decisions are made simply on the judge's personal view of what seems fair under the circumstances (even if the judge doesn't take the time to fully understand the circumstances, and even if he or she has a strange idea of fairness). The judge will then find some way to try to justify his or her decision, even if it means distorting or ignoring the existing law.

The system is slow. Even lawyers get frustrated at how long it can take to get a case completed. Things generally take longer than you would expect. Patience is required to get through the system with a minimum of stress. Don't get angry and let your frustration show.

No two cases are alike. If your friends or co-workers learn that you've filed for bankruptcy, you can be sure you will be getting much "legal" advice from them. *Don't listen to them!* Everyone has their own experience to relate, or a story to tell about a friend or relative who has gone through bankruptcy. *Don't listen to them!* They probably used an attorney, and attorneys are not always clear when explaining the law and procedure to their clients.

After reading this book, you will know more about bankruptcy than many of your friends. Also, your case is not exactly the same as the one they will want to tell you about, so you can't expect your experience will be the same.

THE PLAYERS

Law and the legal system are often compared to games, and just like games, it is important to understand who the players are.

The judge. The judge has the power to determine whether your debts can be discharged (or whether your payment plan can be accepted). In bankruptcy court, the judge is a U.S. District Court Judge, who is appointed to his position for life by the President. Bankruptcy judges have large caseloads, and like it best when your case can be conducted quickly and without hassles. This means that you want to be sure that your papers are completed correctly, with complete and accurate information. Most likely, you will only see the judge at your final hearing, which will only take a few minutes.

The most important thing is to show respect for the judge. This means that you will answer the judge's questions as simply and to the point as possible. Under no circumstances will you get into an argument with the judge, or with a creditor while you are before the judge. You will always follow the judge's instructions without argument or complaint.

The court clerk. The job of the clerk is to handle the filing of papers, the scheduling of hearings, and the maintaining of the court's files. Be sure you are friendly and cooperative toward the people in the clerk's office. If you make a clerk your enemy there is no end to the trouble he or she can cause you.

Generally, the clerk has no interest in the outcome of your case, but is only interested that all of the paperwork is in order. The clerk has the power to accept or reject your papers. If the clerk wants something changed in your papers, just find out what he or she wants, and do it.

If you happen to come across a particularly unfriendly clerk—try to understand that clerks frequently deal with frustrated, angry and rude people. You'll get much better treatment by showing the clerk that you are happy to cooperate and are patient with the slowness of the system, rather than being just another rude person causing him or her stress.

The trustee. After you file your first papers, your case will be assigned to a trustee. The trustee's job is to make sure that your papers are complete and accurate, assure that all of your creditors are notified about your bankruptcy, handle the disposition of your assets, and generally assure that your case continues properly and is ready for final hearing with the judge. The trustee works for the court, and is a middle-person between you, your creditors, and the court.

The creditors. These are the people and companies that you owe money. These people will not be happy about your bankruptcy, because it means they will probably not get paid. Some of them may get to take back the property they sold you, and some of them will get nothing. Some of them may be very hostile, and some of them will just accept your bankruptcy as part of the risk of doing business (after all, they encouraged you to buy on credit).

Once you file for bankruptcy your creditors can no longer bother you for payment. You may stop making payments once you file, except on items you don't want to lose (such as your home and car). All your creditor can do is either object to the court that you don't qualify for bankruptcy, or object to your plan for how their debt is to be handled. In most cases, neither objection meets with much success.

Lawyers. This either refers to your lawyer (which will be discussed more in Section 4 of this book), or to your creditor's lawyer. Generally, in bankruptcy proceedings there will be little difference between dealing with your creditor or his attorney. Many lawyers are dignified and polite in their dealings with the other side in a case. These lawyers will try to get the best deal for their client, and will do it in a polite and honest, but firm and business-like, manner.

Other lawyers are truly nasty people, who are impolite and cannot deal with their opponent in a civilized manner. They will not hesitate to make threats and lie in an attempt to intimidate you. These lawyers simply cannot be reasoned with, and you should not try.

If you encounter one of these lawyers, simply do not speak to him or her. Just address all of your statements to the trustee or the judge instead (very respectfully and politely of course). If you are uncertain of the law as stated by such an attorney, you may wish to consult an attorney yourself.

BANKRUPTCY LAW AND PROCEDURE

This section will give you a summary of the law and the procedure of bankruptcy. We will get into the details and the "how to" later, but first it is important to get a more general overview of the process.

IN GENERAL   The idea of the bankruptcy law is to give you a fresh start, free from your previous debts, with enough assets to live on and get you started again. The law sets up different classes of debts and property, which determine what property you can keep, what property you can't keep, and whether and how much your creditors get paid.

SIX-YEAR   There are some limits as to how often you can use bankruptcy. You may
LIMITATION   not file under Chapter 7 if:

- you obtained a discharge under a Chapter 7, 11, 12 or 13 petition filed within the past six years;

- you had a Chapter 7 case dismissed within the past 180 days because you violated a court order; or,

- you had a Chapter 7 case dismissed within the past 180 days because you asked for dismissal after a creditor asked for the automatic stay to be lifted.

However, these limits do not apply to Chapter 13 cases, which may be filed at any time. If your secured debts exceed $350,000, or your unsecured debts exceed $100,000, you may not use Chapter 13. If you are in this situation, you should consult a lawyer about the possibility of filing under Chapter 11 of the Bankruptcy Code.

EXEMPT AND NON-EXEMPT PROPERTY

Each piece of property you own will be classified as either *exempt* (which means you may be able to keep it), or as *non-exempt* (which means you will have to turn it over to the trustee). Although the Bankruptcy Code is a federal law, the available exemptions are different in each state. Appendix A of this book will tell you how to determine the property that is exempt in your state, and this will be discussed in more detail later.

Most states will allow you to keep a certain dollar value of:

- real estate;

- a car;

- tools used in your profession;

- insurance policies;

- clothing;

- household furnishings;

- retirement benefits;

- public benefits (such as workers' compensation and unemployment); and other personal items.

These are exempt property. However, exempt property may still be lost if you borrowed money to buy it and don't keep up your payments.

SECURED AND UNSECURED DEBTS

This brings us to the classification of debts as either *secured* or *unsecured*. A *secured debt* is one that is covered by a certain piece of property. The most common examples are home mortgages and car loans. The papers you signed when you borrowed the money specifically state that if you do not pay, the lender may take the property. You may not keep such property unless you pay for it, even if it would otherwise be exempt property in your state. So, if you do not want to lose your home or car, you will have to arrange a payment plan acceptable to your lender, or just keep your payments current.

An *unsecured debt* is not covered by any property. Examples of unsecured debts are a department store credit card, a VISA card, and medical bills. In these cases, the lender does not get paid and does not get any property either. Even if you bought your dining room furniture with your credit card, it is still an unsecured debt (unless you also signed some additional paper that states that the property secured the loan).

MORTGAGE
FORECLOSURES

Since a mortgage is a secured debt, filing for bankruptcy will not allow you to keep your home without paying for it. The best a bankruptcy can do is buy you time to make arrangements to catch up on your payments, or allow you to arrange some kind of adjustment in the terms of your loan so that you can keep your home.

When you file for bankruptcy, the law imposes what is called an *automatic stay*. This prevents any creditor from taking any legal action against you unless they first get the permission of the bankruptcy court. Therefore, if your lender has already begun a *foreclosure action*, filing bankruptcy will temporarily stop the foreclosure; probably for a few weeks at most. If your lender has not yet filed for foreclosure, it may not do so until the bankruptcy court lifts the automatic stay.

If you file under Chapter 7 of the Bankruptcy Code, you will either need to bring your payments current or work out some arrangement with your lender by the time the automatic stay is lifted. If you file for bankruptcy under Chapter 13 of the Bankruptcy Code, you may be able to get the bankruptcy court to require the lender to accept new terms for repayment (such as extending the time of the loan and lowering the payments). The best thing to do is to talk to your lender as soon as you find you are having trouble making payments. The longer you wait, the less likely you are to be able to work something out.

When you talk to your lender, explain your financial situation and have a plan to present (such as extending the term of the loan and lowering your monthly payments). Just be sure you can follow through with the plan you propose. Many lenders would rather work with you than fore-close. For a lender, foreclosure is time-consuming and expensive; and they really would rather not have to hassle with taking the home back and trying to resell it for enough to recoup their costs.

NON-DISCHARGEABLE DEBTS

One other significant part of the law is that there are a few types of debts that cannot be discharged in bankruptcy. The four most common types of non-dischargeable debts are—taxes (with certain exceptions), government guaranteed student loans, child support, and alimony. So even if you go through a bankruptcy, you will still have to pay these debts.

BANKRUPTCY PROCEDURE

The bankruptcy procedure can be viewed as a simple four-step process:

1. You prepare and file your VOLUNTARY PETITION and various supporting documents. (see form 1, p.165.) This is simply a request for the court to discharge your debts (or approve your payment plan) according to the law, and information about your income, expenses, property and debts.

2. The trustee sends notices to all of your creditors to advise them that you have filed for bankruptcy. This gives them an opportunity to be sure you have given correct information in your VOLUNTARY PETITION, and to raise any questions or objections.

3. You have a meeting with the trustee and your creditors. This is when any questions or objections are discussed and settled.

4. You attend a hearing, at which time the judge will discharge your debts (or approve your payment plan). This may even be a mass-discharge of many cases at one time, in which you and many others obtain a discharge at the same time.

OTHER
CONSIDERATIONS

You should also consider the following things before you decide to file for bankruptcy:

- If a friend or relative co-signed a loan for you, that friend or relative will still be liable for the debt.

- You may have your case dismissed if the judge determines that you have enough income to pay your debts, if you defrauded your creditors, or if you charged a lot for entertainment, vacations, or luxury items just before filing.

- You may not need to file for bankruptcy if your only goal is to get bill collectors off your back, or to avoid having your property or wages attached. Other state and federal laws may be able to accomplish these goals without filing for bankruptcy.

CHAPTER 7
BANKRUPTCY
(DISCHARGE OF
DEBTS)

As mentioned earlier, there are two types of bankruptcy for individuals: the discharge of debts, and the payment plan. Chapter 7 of the Bankruptcy Code is for the discharge of debts, which is the traditional bankruptcy. This is where you either pay for, or give up, your property for secured debts. You will surrender any non-exempt property in order to pay off as much of your other debt as possible. You will keep all of your other exempt property, and will be forever released from any obligation to repay the remaining debt.

One important requirement for a Chapter 7 bankruptcy is that you don't have enough income to allow you to pay your debts. If the judge finds that you have enough income, he will dismiss your case. This will be discussed in more detail in Section 3 of this book.

CHAPTER 13
BANKRUPTCY
(PAYMENT PLAN)

In a Chapter 13 bankruptcy you are not seeking to get rid of all of your debt entirely, but only to do one or a combination of the following:

1. restructure your payments so that they are more manageable considering your income;

2. get rid of part of your debt so that you can manage payments again.

This can be done by spreading your payments over a longer period of time, or by paying only a part of the loan. Either way your monthly or weekly payment will be reduced. This type of payment plan can last up to three years, which means your finances will be under the watchful eye of the trustee during this time.

The two main things the trustee and the judge will consider in deciding whether to accept your plan are:

1. whether the creditors are being treated fairly and

2. whether each creditor will receive at least as much as if you had gone with the traditional Chapter 7 bankruptcy.

For a Chapter 13 bankruptcy you will fill out some different forms than for a Chapter 7. The main difference is that you will need to fill out a form in which you offer a payment plan that you create. In a Chapter 13 case the creditors' meeting is usually concerned with trying to reach a plan that will be acceptable to the creditors. So you may spend some time negotiating with the creditors as they try to get you to change your plan so they get more money or get it faster.

It is not necessary that the creditors agree with your plan, but if they do agree, it will be easily accepted by the trustee and the judge.

Even if the creditors object to your plan, it will still be approved as long as it is fair (in the judge's opinion of what is fair, which usually relates to all creditors of the same type being treated equally), and as long as each creditor gets at least as much as if you had filed under Chapter 7.

CONVERTING TO ANOTHER CHAPTER

It is also possible for you to convert to a Chapter 7 bankruptcy, if you later determine this is a better solution to your debt problems. It is also possible to convert a Chapter 7 to a Chapter 13 case, although this is not usually done unless the judge determines that you have enough income to pay off your debts over a few years and is about to dismiss your case.

Most people will find that they have less income to go around, therefore requiring a Chapter 7. Only if you find that your income is sufficient to enable you to pay off most of your debts within three years would you consider changing to a Chapter 13.

LAWYERS 2

You are not required to have a lawyer in order to file for bankruptcy. Most people should be able to handle their own bankruptcy. You will probably need an attorney if:

- you are involved in a business, either alone or in a partnership;

- you own stock in a privately held corporation;

- you are married and your spouse is not filing for bankruptcy with you;

- you are a farmer (there are special bankruptcy laws covering farm bankruptcy.); or,

- you encounter a creditor, trustee, or judge who is particularly difficult.

NEEDING A LAWYER

No doubt, one of your first questions about bankruptcy is: How much will an attorney cost? Attorneys come in all price ranges. Most attorneys will charge between $750 and $1,500, depending upon where you live and the complexity of your case. Ads for $150 to $200 bankruptcies are usually only available in very simple cases, and are "no frills" services. If you use one of these lawyers, just be sure you know exactly what will be provided for the fee. The lawyer will usually want to be paid in advance. Most new (and therefore less expensive) attorneys would be quite capable of handling a simple bankruptcy, but, by the time you've read this book, you will probably know as much about bankruptcy as most of these new attorneys.

ADVANTAGES TO
HAVING A
LAWYER

The following are some reasons why you may want to consider hiring a lawyer:

- You may be able to save more of your property. A lawyer may be able to find more loopholes in the bankruptcy law, or give you other suggestions, which will preserve more assets or discharge more debt. However, these savings may be offset by the attorney's fee you will need to pay. Generally, the more loopholes you want, the more experienced (and expensive) of an attorney you will need.

- Judges and other attorneys may take you more seriously. People who represent themselves often waste time by being unfamiliar with the procedures. However, this should not be a problem with anyone who has read this book.

- A lawyer can serve as a buffer between you and your creditors.

- In the event your case becomes complicated, it is an advantage to have an attorney who is familiar with your case. It can be comforting to have a lawyer for advice and reassurance. Again, the more advice and reassurance, the higher the attorney's fee will rise.

ADVANTAGES TO
REPRESENTING
YOURSELF

Here are some reasons why you may want to do the work yourself:

- You save the cost of a lawyer.

- Sometimes judges and trustees feel more sympathetic toward a person who is not represented by a lawyer. Often they will actually help you.

- The procedure may be faster. One of the most frequent complaints about lawyers involves delay in completing the case, usually due to heavy caseloads. If you are handling your own case, you will be able to keep it moving through the system.

- Selecting a good attorney is not easy.

MIDDLE
GROUND

You may want to look for an attorney who will be willing to accept an hourly fee to answer your questions and give you help on an as-needed basis. Expect to pay at least $75 per hour for such consultation. Attorneys offering "free initial consultation," or a consultation "for just $20," will often not provide you with any usable advice, or explain how you should do something.

SELECTING A LAWYER

If you decide that you wish a lawyer to represent you in filing for bankruptcy, or even in dealing with your creditors to try to avoid bankruptcy, you will need to seek out a lawyer. The lawyer you select should be experienced in bankrupcty, should instill confidence in you, and should be someone you feel comfortable talking with about your situation. This section will help you in locating such a lawyer.

FINDING LAWYERS

Finding a lawyer is a two-step process. First, you need to decide which attorney (or attorneys) to make an appointment with. Second, you need to decide if you want to hire that attorney.

Ask a friend. A common, and frequently the best, way to find a lawyer is to ask someone you know to recommend one.

Lawyer Referral Service. You can find a referral service by looking in the Yellow Pages of your phone directory under the heading "Attorney Referral Services" or "Attorneys." The referral service is free, but it does not guarantee the quality of the attorney's work, nor the level of experience or ability.

Yellow Pages. Check under the heading for "Attorneys." Look for ads for firms or lawyers that indicate they handle bankruptcy or credit matters.

Newspaper. In the classified ads you should find a section for "Legal Services," that often includes the least expensive attorneys. But expect minimal services. You may even be given a set of forms to complete yourself.

Ask another lawyer. If you have used an attorney in the past (such as for a will, real estate closing or traffic ticket), call him or her and ask for a referral to a bankruptcy attorney.

EVALUATING A LAWYER

You should select three to five lawyers worthy of further consideration. Call each attorney's office and ask the following questions:

- Does the attorney (or firm) handle bankruptcies?

- How much can you expect it to cost?

- How soon can you get an appointment?

- What is the cost for an initial consultation?

If you like the answers you get, ask if you can speak to the attorney. Once you get in contact with the attorney (either by phone or at an appointment), ask the following questions:

- How much will it cost?

- How will the fee be paid? (Usually it is paid in advance, in full.)

- What percentage of the attorney's cases involve bankruptcies? (Do not expect an exact answer, but you should get a rough estimate of at least 10%.)

- How long will it take? (Do not expect an exact answer, but the attorney should be able to give you an average range and discuss the variables.)

If you get acceptable answers to these questions, it is time to ask yourself these questions:

- Do I feel comfortable talking to this lawyer?

- Does this lawyer seem confident?

- Is this lawyer willing and able to explain things so I can understand?

If you get satisfactory answers to all of these questions, you probably have a lawyer you will be able to work with. Remember, you are interviewing the lawyer to see if you want to hire him.

WORKING WITH A LAWYER

You will most likely work best with your attorney if you keep an open, honest and friendly attitude. You should also consider the following suggestions.

ASK QUESTIONS   If you want to know something, or if you do not understand something, ask your attorney. If you do not understand the answer, ask him or her to explain it again. There are many points of law that even lawyers do not fully understand, so you should not be embarrassed to ask questions. If your lawyer won't take the time to explain what he or she is doing, it may be time to look for a new lawyer.

GIVE YOUR LAWYER
COMPLETE INFORMATION

Anything you tell your lawyer is confidential, and your lawyer cannot help you if he or she does not have all of the information.

ACCEPT
REALITY

Accept what your lawyer tells you about the law and the system. It is pointless to argue because the law or the system does not work the way you think it should. Remember, it is not your lawyer's fault that the system is not perfect, or that the law does not say what you would like it to say.

BE PATIENT

Be patient with the system, as well as with your attorney. Do not expect your attorney to return your phone call within an hour. Your attorney may not be able to return it the same day either. Most lawyers are very busy. It is rare that an attorney can maintain a full caseload and still make each client feel as if he is the only client.

TALK TO THE
SECRETARY

Your lawyer's secretary can be a valuable source of information. So be friendly and get to know him or her. Often the secretary will be able to answer your questions and you will not get a bill for the time you talk. Even if the secretary can't answer your question, he or she can probably get the answer from the attorney and call you back faster than if you insist on waiting to speak directly to the lawyer.

BE ON TIME

Be on time to appointments with your lawyer, and to court hearings.

KEEP YOUR
CASE MOVING

Many lawyers operate on the old principal of "the squeaking wheel gets the oil." Work on a case tends to get put off until a deadline is near, an emergency develops, or the client calls. There is a reason for this. Many lawyers take more cases than can be effectively handled in order to increase their income. Your task is to become a squeaking wheel, but one that does not squeak to the point of being aggravating to your lawyer and his or her office staff. Whenever you talk to your lawyer, ask him or her the following questions:

- What is the next step?

- When do you expect it to be done?

- When should I talk to you next?

If you do not hear from the lawyer when you expect, call him or her the following day. Do not remind your lawyer that you did not receive a call; just ask how your case is going.

TRY TO SAVE MONEY

Of course you do not want to spend unnecessary money for an attorney. Here are a few things you can do to avoid excess legal fees:

- Don't make unnecessary phone calls to your lawyer.

- Give information to the secretary whenever possible.

- Direct questions to the secretary first.

- Plan phone calls so you get to the point. Write down an outline if necessary.

- Do some of the legwork yourself—pick up and deliver papers, for example. Ask what you can do to assist your lawyer.

- Be prepared for appointments. Have all related papers with you, plan your visit to get to the point. Make an outline of what you want to discuss and ask.

FIRING YOUR LAWYER

If you find that you can no longer work with your lawyer, or do not trust your lawyer, it is time to either go it alone or get a new attorney. You will need to send your lawyer a letter stating that you no longer desire his or her services and are discharging him or her from your case. Also state that you will be coming by his or her office the following day to pick up your file.

The attorney does not have to give you his or her own notes or other work in progress, but your lawyer must give you the essential contents of your file (such as copies of papers already prepared and billed for, and any documents you provided). If your attorney refuses to give you your file for any reason, contact your state's bar association about filing a complaint or *grievance* against the lawyer. Of course, you will need to settle any remaining fees owed.

AVOIDING BANKRUPTCY 3

Before resigning to the fact that bankruptcy is the only option for you, there are things you may want to consider. Perhaps there is a way for you to work with your creditors and avoid bankruptcy altogether. The first part of this section demonstrates that there are some good reasons to avoid bankruptcy. There are also, however, good reasons to file for bankruptcy, in the right circumstances. The second part of this section will help you determine if the circumstances are right.

THE EFFECTS OF BANKRUPTCY

Bankruptcy should be regarded as a last resort. Before you jump into a bankruptcy, it is a good idea to evaluate your financial situation, and consider the effects of a bankruptcy. Before you make a final decision, be sure to look at Section 8 of this book to see if any of the special circumstances discussed there apply to you.

FINANCIAL EFFECTS

A bankruptcy is a mixed blessing. It will have both positive and negative financial effects. These can be divided into immediate and long-term effects.

Immediate effects. An immediate positive effect is that your creditors will get off your back. However, this may only last a short time for certain kinds of debts. Such things as utility cut-offs, mortgage fore-closures, or evictions, may only be delayed for a few days or weeks. Once you file for bankruptcy, your financial dealings come under the scrutiny of the bankruptcy trustee. You will need his permission to sell any assets or to pay any debts.

Long-term effects. These are the effects after your bankruptcy is completed. The fact that you now have a bankruptcy in your history will make it difficult for you to obtain credit. This will affect your ability to qualify for a mortgage, buy a car, or obtain a credit card. It is a long, gradual process to build up credit once you've declared bankruptcy.

It may also make it difficult for you to get a promotion or be given a position of trust at work, or to get hired by a new employer who does a credit check. You will probably also be starting over with fewer possessions than you had before your bankruptcy. Some of your property will probably get repossessed, and some of it may have to be sold. If a relative or friend co-signed a loan for you, that relative or friend will still be liable to repay the loan.

A bankruptcy may also cause you to lose your retirement benefits. Be sure to read Section 8 of this book for more information on pension plans and how they are affected by bankruptcy.

You will have to be very careful not to get into debt problems again. You can only file for bankruptcy once every six years.

EMOTIONAL
EFFECTS
In addition to the financial effects, most people experience some emotional effects when they file for bankruptcy.

Yourself. You may experience a feeling of failure or dishonesty. Failure because you couldn't manage your affairs better, or were not smart enough to handle your money; dishonesty because you feel you are cheating your creditors. Although there are many logical arguments for not feeling this way, many people still cannot overcome the feeling on an emotional level.

The following categories are separate in some respects, but they are also part of how you see yourself. Regardless of how others really feel about your situation, you will see and interpret their reaction in terms of how you feel about yourself.

Your family and friends. If you are married, your spouse, and possibly your children, will have to know about the bankruptcy. You will need to prepare for how you will discuss it with them. You may also have to be prepared to deal with their feelings of failure, disappointment, and guilt. There may also be extended family members involved, such as parents, brothers, aunts and uncles, and friends. These people may or may not understand and sympathize with your situation.

Your employer. It is possible that you can keep your bankruptcy out of your workplace, but it is not likely. Although your employer probably won't admit it, a bankruptcy may affect your ability to obtain promotions, or to be entrusted with certain responsibilities (such as handling money or accounts). Of course, the same thing may happen if you do not file, and a creditor files a wage garnishment.

For some, or all, of these reasons you should first explore whether you might avoid bankruptcy.

INCOME AND EXPENSE WORKSHEET

In order to be considering bankruptcy, you must be in a situation where your income is not sufficient to cover your monthly expenses. To find out just how bad your situation is we will examine your current budget. Complete the INCOME AND EXPENSE WORKSHEET in Appendix C. (see worksheet 1, p.159.) Following these guidelines:

- Be sure to use *monthly* amounts in completing this form.

- To convert a weekly amount, multiply the amount by 4.3.

- To convert a bi-weekly amount, divide by 2, then multiply the answer by 4.3.

The following relates to the INCOME portion of form 1:

☞ Take Home Pay: This refers to your total pay after you deduct for taxes and social security. If you have other payroll deductions, such as for a medical or dental plan, uniforms, or savings plan, they should be listed under the EXPENSES section of this form. Therefore, add these deductions back to the take home pay shown on your paycheck. If your pay changes from paycheck to paycheck, obtain an average by dividing your yearly income by 12, or by some other appropriate method.

☞ Self Employment Income: Calculate an average monthly income if you are self-employed (either as your main job or as a second job). Consult a book that covers business bankruptcies, or see a lawyer, if you are self-employed and are incorporated, and have employees or a financially complex business operation.

☞ Interest and Dividends: This includes such things as interest on bank accounts, certificates of deposit (CDs), stocks, bonds, mutual funds, etc.

☞ Income from Real Estate: This is income from any rental property you own.

☞ Retirement Income: This includes pensions and other retirement payments from your prior employment.

☞ Alimony or Support Payments: This includes money you receive as alimony, maintenance, child support, etc. Only count these payments if you receive them on a fairly regular and dependable basis.

☞ Other: This might include such things as Social Security, unemployment compensation, disability benefits, welfare benefits, or income from loans you made to other people.

The following relates to the EXPENSES section of form 1:

☞ Homeowners/Renter's Insurance: If homeowners insurance is included in your mortgage payment, it should not be listed here again. If you rent and have renters insurance on your possessions, you will be paying it separately from your rent payment, so list it here.

☞ Real Estate Taxes: If these are included in your mortgage payment, they should not be listed here again.

☞ Other Installment Loan Payments: This relates to all loans except your mortgage and auto loan payments. This will include such things as credit cards, home equity loans, boat loans, vacation loans, home improvement loans, and swimming pool loans.

NOTE: *The remaining items of the form are self-explanatory. Just make sure everything is converted to a* **monthly** *amount.*

☞ Next, add all of your monthly income and write the total in the space for TOTAL MONTHLY INCOME. Add all of your monthly expenses and write the total in the space for TOTAL MONTHLY EXPENSES.

☞ Finally, subtract the total expenses from the total income and write the amount in the space for DEFICIT. This should give you a negative number, which will tell you how much money you are falling short by each month. (If you get a positive number, then you have either forgotten to list some of your expenses, or you are making enough money to meet your monthly expenses and should not be thinking about bankruptcy.)

PROPERTY WORKSHEET

To put it simply, *property* is something you own (such as money, a house, a car, furniture, etc.), and a *debt* is money you owe. Property may also be referred to as an *asset*. The two things you will consider in trying to avoid bankruptcy are whether you can cut your expenses, and whether you can sell some assets and pay off some debts. First, it is necessary to explain the types of property and debts involved in a bankruptcy. Then, we will discuss some general guidelines for determining whether bankruptcy is right for you. Finally, we will discuss what can be done to try to avoid bankruptcy.

Property is divided into *exempt* and *non-exempt* categories. Remember, the purpose of bankruptcy is to help you start over financially. It would not be helpful to leave you without property, so the bankruptcy laws allow you to keep a certain amount of your property. The types and amounts of property you are allowed to keep are exempt property. The type and amount of property that is exempt is a matter of state law (and alternative federal law in some states).

Although the Bankruptcy Code is a federal law, the question of exempt property is generally determined by your state government. Generally, most states exempt the following types of property, at least up to a certain value or amount:

- motor vehicles;

- clothing and personal effects;

- household furnishings;

- tools used in your trade or profession;

- equity in a home;

- life insurance;

- public employee pensions (See Section 8 of this book.); or,

- social security, welfare, unemployment or workers' compensation, or other public benefits accumulated in a bank account.

Typical examples of non-exempt property are:

- the above items over a certain amount;

- a second car;

- a boat or recreational vehicle;

- a vacation home;

- cash, bank accounts, certificates of deposit; or

- other investments, such as stocks, bonds, coin collections, etc.

The **PROPERTY WORKSHEET** in Appendix C, which you will fill out next will divide your property into exempt and non-exempt categories. (see worksheet 2, p.160.) If you live in Arkansas, Connecticut, the District of Columbia, Hawaii, Massachusetts, Michigan, Minnesota, New Jersey, New Mexico, Pennsylvania, Rhode Island, South Carolina, Texas, Vermont, Washington, or Wisconsin, you have the following choices in determining what property is exempt:

1. Use the exemptions listed for your state *and* the Federal Non-Bankruptcy Exemptions, both of which are listed in Appendix A of this book. (If you use your state exemptions, you may *not* use any of the Federal Bankruptcy Exemptions.)

2. Use the Federal Bankruptcy Exemptions *and* the Federal Non-bankruptcy Exemptions, both of which are listed in Appendix A of this book. (If you use the Federal Bankruptcy Exemptions, you may *not* use any of your state exemptions.)

If you live in any other state, you may only use your state exemptions and the Federal Non-Bankruptcy Exemptions.

> *Warning:* Even if the property is exempt, you may still lose the property if it is tied to a secured debt. For example: Your home is exempt property under your state's laws. If you borrowed money from a bank to buy the house, and the bank holds a mortgage on the house, the bank can still foreclose and take your house if you do not pay.

The **PROPERTY WORKSHEET** is divided into six columns, each of which have both a number and a title. The following instructions refer to each column by number. (see worksheet 2, p.160.)

☞ In column (1), list all of your property. Do not list anything in more than one category. For each category of property in worksheet 2, check if any such items are exempt on your state's list in Appendix A of this book. If so, be sure to list those items separately.

Example: If your state exempts wedding rings, be sure to list your wedding rings as a separate item in the Jewelry category in worksheet 2.

If you live in Arkansas, Connecticut, the District of Columbia, Hawaii, Massachusetts, Michigan, Minnesota, New Jersey, New Mexico, Pennsylvania, Rhode Island, South Carolina, Texas, Vermont, Washington, or Wisconsin, you should also compare your state's exemptions with the Federal Bankruptcy Exemptions at the beginning of Appendix A. Also Column (1) is divided into several categories of property, as follows:

- Real Estate: List any real estate you own, by each property's address or other brief description.

- Autos: Include cars, trucks, motorcycles, etc.

- Boats: Include boats, engines, boating equipment, as well as any other recreational vehicles.

- Cash on hand: This is cash in your pocket, wallet, purse, mattress, etc. It does not include money in a bank.

- Bank accounts: This is where you list all of your bank accounts, by your bank name and account number.

- Clothing: You can just give an estimate of the total value of your clothing. Only list specific items if they have great value (such as a mink coat, or original designer items).

- Jewelry: Costume jewelry need not be listed by item, but gold, diamonds and other precious metals and gems should be listed by each item.

- Household goods: This includes all of your furniture, pots and pans, dishes, personal items, etc. A general estimate can be given for most things. Although any items of great value should be listed separately, but first check to see it they fit in one of the other categories in this form.

- Collections: This is for such things as coins, stamps, paintings, books, and other valuable collectibles.

- Sports equipment: Include firearms, pool tables, golf clubs, etc.

- Business goods/Trade tools: This includes any such items you need in order to conduct your business or to engage in your occupation.

- Investments: This includes any stocks, bonds, patents, copyrights, licenses, etc.

- Insurance: This includes any cash value in life insurance policies, annuities, etc.

- Other property: This is where you list anything that doesn't fit into one of the other categories. Again, be sure to check your state's listing in Appendix A.

☞ Column (2) is titled VALUE. Fill in the approximate value of each of the items of property you listed under Column (1). For some items you will know the exact value, and for others you will have to make a good estimate. For such things as autos and boats you may be able to find a *blue book* (which may be any color) at your local library or at a local dealer, which will give approximate values. For other items, such as clothing, personal belongings and furniture, just estimate what you think you could sell these items for at a garage sale. Estimate low, but do not get ridiculous.

☞ Column (3) is used to fill in how much money, if any, you still owe on any of the items listed under Column (1). For the purposes of this form, you only *owe* something if the item can be foreclosed on or repossessed if you fail to pay.

Example: If you bought your dining set with your VISA card, it cannot be repossessed. Therefore, you do not owe anything on the dining set.

☛ Next, subtract the amount owed in Column (3) from the value in Column (2), and write in the difference in Column (4). This will give you your equity in each piece of property. *Equity* is the amount of cash you would have if you sold the property and paid off the amount you owe.

☛ For Column (5), refer to your state's listing in Appendix A, where you will find a list of the items and amounts that are exempt. Also look at the beginning of Appendix A to see if you are in a state that permits use of the Federal Bankruptcy Exemptions. If so, compare the state and Federal Bankruptcy Exemptions to see which would make more of your property exempt.

The state exemptions will usually give you a better result, but not always. If you will get more exempt property under the Federal Bankruptcy Exemptions, use them instead of the state exemptions. For each item of property, you may find that item completely exempt, or only exempt to a certain value. The following examples will help illustrate this point:

Example 1: If you live in Florida, the home you live in (your *homestead*) is completely exempt, no matter what its value. If you have a home worth $100,000, it is fully exempt. This means you don't have to sell your house to pay off your creditors. (But if you have a mortgage, then you have to make your payments.)

Example 2: If you live in Illinois, only $7,500 of the value of your home is exempt. If your home is worth $100,000, you may only claim an exemption of $7,500. You would have to sell your home, or take out a new mortgage for $92,500 so that your equity is only $7,500. Of course you would have to pay your mortgage payments, if you could get a loan with your financial problems. Illinois does not allow the Federal Bankruptcy Exemptions, so you can only exempt the $7,500 allowed by Illinois.

Example 3: If you live in New Jersey, your home is not exempt at all. Whether your equity is $100,000 or $1.00, you would lose it in a bankruptcy if you use the New Jersey exemptions.. However, New Jersey allows you to use the alternative Federal Bankruptcy Exemptions, which would allow you to keep up to $15,000 in a home.

Look at your available exemptions in Appendix A and determine what property is exempt. Fill in the amount of the exemption in Column (5).

☛ In Column (6), place a check mark beside each item of property for which the debt is secured. (If necessary, re-read the part of this section on secured and unsecured debts.) If the debt for that property is secured, you will need to keep up your payment, or at least work out something with the creditor, in order to keep the property (even if the property is exempt in your state).

☛ Write the totals of each column at the bottom.

DEBT ASSESSMENT

The next step is to assess how much money you owe and the kinds of debts you have.

DISCHARGEABLE AND NON-DISCHARGEABLE DEBTS

In a bankruptcy, debts are first divided into two types: *dischargeable* and *non-dischargeable*. A dischargeable debt is one that the bankruptcy laws allow you to discharge, or cancel. The best examples of dischargeable debts are the money you owe on credit cards, such as a Visa, Mastercard, or department store card, and medical bills. Most consumer debts are dischargeable in bankruptcy, and these are the types of debts that lead most people into a situation that requires them to file for bankruptcy.

If you have several credit cards, and you charge them all up to the limit, it is easy to get in over your head. It is easy to recall cases in which an individual, or more often a young couple, has charged as much as $15,000. And that was in addition to their mortgage payment and car payment!

A non-dischargeable debt is one that you will still owe after the bankruptcy is completed. Examples of non-dischargeable debts are:

- student loans;

- child support;

- alimony obligations;

- delinquent taxes;

- some court-ordered judgments; or,

- debts arising from fraud (such as from providing false credit application information, from theft, or from obtaining credit with the intention of filing for bankruptcy to avoid payment).

SECURED AND UNSECURED DEBTS

Debts are also divided into two other categories: *secured* and *unsecured*. A secured debt is one that can be viewed as *attached* to a particular piece of property. The prime example of a secured debt is a mortgage. The mortgage means that, if you do not pay the money you borrowed to buy your house, the lender can take your house. Most car loans also include a *financing statement*, which is essentially the same as a mortgage. If you do not pay, the lender gets your car.

However, most credit card loans are unsecured. They are not tied to any particular piece of property. If you do not pay, the bank cannot grab your property (at least not without going to all of the trouble of suing you and trying to attach your property later).

DEBT WORKSHEET (WORKSHEET 3)

Now, complete the DEBT WORKSHEET in Appendix C according to the following guidelines. (see worksheet 3, p.161.) This form is divided into six columns, five of which are numbered. The first column is to remind you of the types of property you have.

☞ In Column (1) list each debt by the lender's name and account number.

☞ In Column (2) list what the loan was for, such as home, car, boat, vacation, etc. For your credit cards you don't need to list each little purchase you made, as the only purpose of this column is to help you remember what the loan is for, and to determine whether the loan is secured by any property.

☞ In Column (3) write down the balance due on each loan. You don't need to have each one exact to the penny, but be as accurate as possible.

☞ In Column (4) write in the same amount as Column (3) for each loan that is secured by a piece of property.

☞ In Column (5) write in the same amount as Column (3) for each loan that is a dischargeable loan. For purposes of worksheet 3, a secured loan is not considered dischargeable, unless you are willing to give up that item of property.

☞ Write the totals of each column at the bottom.

GENERAL GUIDELINES

In order to determine whether you should file for bankruptcy, you need to evaluate your situation according to the following four factors:

1. Can you reduce your total monthly payments so that you can manage things on your income?

2. How much of your debt is dischargeable?

3. How much of your debt is secured by your property?

4. How much of your property is exempt?

Once you have done this, you can get a good idea of whether you can avoid bankruptcy and where things would stand after a bankruptcy. You will be able to estimate how much property you would be able to keep, and how much money you would still owe to creditors.

Look at your monthly budget first [refer to your completed INCOME AND EXPENSE WORKSHEET (worksheet 1)]. Examine each of your monthly expenses.

- Are there any that you can reduce or eliminate?

- Can you sell some of your property to pay off some of your debts?

- Can you move to a cheaper apartment, or sell your home and find an apartment that will reduce your monthly housing costs?

- Can you sell your late model car and buy a less expensive one?

This is no time to think about maintaining your lifestyle. After all, it may be your lifestyle that got you into financial trouble in the first place. If you can make such adjustments to your expenses, you may be able to avoid bankruptcy. If such adjustments still will not help your situation, continue on to the next paragraph and look at the types of debts and property you have.

A general rule of thumb is that if you can discharge more than 50% of your debts, a Chapter 7 bankruptcy would probably improve your financial situation. To determine if your situation fits this guideline, refer to worksheet 3, take the total of Column (3) and divide it by 2. If the answer is equal to or less than the total of Column (5), you can probably benefit from a Chapter 7 bankruptcy. If the answer is greater than the total of Column (5), you may benefit from a Chapter 13 bankruptcy, or even avoid bankruptcy.

Be sure to read the next section on Alternatives to Bankruptcy. Following the instructions on planning a budget will help you to better understand your situation, even if you already know that you need to file for bankruptcy.

ALTERNATIVES TO BANKRUPTCY

If, after filling out worksheets 1, 2, and 3 from Appendix C of this book, it looks as if you may be able to avoid bankruptcy, this section will present some ideas for how you can get your debt problems under control. Of course, the first step is to *stop charging*.

CREDIT COUNSELING

If you would like to totally avoid bankruptcy, you may want to see a credit counselor.

> ***Warning***: Beware of private *debt counselors* or offers for *debt consolidation* loans. Such "help" often only results in one large payment instead of many smaller payments, and you will still have trouble making that monthly payment. Furthermore, such operations charge counseling fees that only further take away needed cash. Soon you may be facing bankruptcy again. Also, *avoid* the now-famous *home equity loan*. This can end up converting your unsecured debts into secured debts, which means that you may not be able to file for bankruptcy without losing your home!

You can feel comfortable going to see a credit counselor who is associated with your local Consumer Credit Counseling Service. This organization can be found in the Yellow Pages telephone directory under the heading "Credit Counseling." This is a non-profit organization set up by creditors, such as banks, department stores, credit card companies and other businesses.

A credit counselor will contact your creditors, help establish new payment arrangements, and help you set up a budget you can handle. However, if you miss payments on your new budget, you may still end up in a bankruptcy, and will have possibly paid hundreds of dollars to your creditors needlessly. In this situation, it would have been better for you to have filed for bankruptcy at the start.

A Consumer Credit Counseling (CCC) plan is similar to a Chapter 13 bankruptcy, but on a less formal basis. It is also cheaper, in that the cost of the CCC assistance is minimal (about $20.00), whereas higher court filing fees and other costs are involved in a Chapter 13 bankruptcy case. It will look better on a credit report to have a record of CCC assistance, than to have a record of a bankruptcy. The main financial difference is that a CCC plan will require you to pay your debts in full, whereas a Chapter 13 may only require payment of a portion of your debts.

If you feel a strong obligation to pay your creditors in full, you should consider paying a visit to your local Consumer Credit Counseling Service office.

BE YOUR OWN CREDIT COUNSELOR

In theory, there is nothing a credit counselor can do that you cannot do. On a practical level, creditors are more inclined to listen to a credit counselor. Your creditors do not want you to file for bankruptcy, because it means they will not get paid in full. Because of this, they should have a strong incentive to be reasonable. Your main goal is to get the creditor to allow you to make smaller payments, over a longer period of time.

Example: George has a $1,500 balance on a credit card from a local department store. His payments are $74.89 a month, and the balance will take two years to pay off. If the department store will agree to accept payments over an additional year, George's monthly payment will be lowered to $54.23 a month. This lowers his monthly payment by $20.66. If he has ten loans like this, he could save over $200 per month, which may be enough to enable him to keep up his payments based on his income.

Planning a budget. The place to begin is by reviewing the INCOME AND EXPENSE WORKSHEET (worksheet 1), that you completed earlier. You will need this form and a calculator to plan your budget. (If you do not have a calculator or adding machine, you will have to do the arithmetic by hand.) The copy of worksheet 1 you completed shows your budget as it is right now. Use a blank copy to start your new budget.

Your total income will remain the same, so write it in under TOTAL MONTHLY INCOME. Enter this amount in your calculator. Now go through all of your expenses, and subtract each one from the TOTAL MONTHLY INCOME figure. First, identify the most important item, which is probably your rent or mortgage payment (unless you are prepared to go live with friends and relatives). Write this amount in the appropriate place on the form, and subtract it from your total income.

Second, identify your next most important expense, and so on. For each item, ask yourself if there is any way to reduce the amount you spend each month. If you can reduce the amount, then use the reduced amount, and subtract it from the total. Your essential payments are for housing (including utilities), food, and transportation (probably your car).

In order to survive and earn a living, you need a place to live, food, and a way to get to and from work. If you are unable to make these essential payments with your income, or are unable to reduce these payments to that level, you may want to apply for some type of public assistance (yes, welfare) in addition to filing for a Chapter 7 bankruptcy.

Once you have subtracted the essential living expenses, you will be left with the total remaining income available to pay your creditors and other expenses. (Absolutely last on your list should be the "Recreation/Travel/Entertainment" expenses.) Now, start subtracting your payments for loans that are secured loans. These are any loans where your property can be repossessed if you don't pay. Most credit card debts are not secured by any particular property. The most common secured loans are for homes (including home equity loans), automobiles, boats, and occasionally furniture. If the only paper you signed was the typical charge card receipt for Visa, Mastercard, Sears, or other department store charges, the loan is not secured.

By now you are probably left with a small amount of income (if any at all), with which you can make payments on the rest of your loans. Add up the remaining loan payments, and subtract them from your remaining income. If your answer is -0- or more, then whatever adjustments you made to your expenses were enough to eliminate your debt problem. Now your only problem is to try to live according to your new budget.

If your answer is less than -0-, however, this is how much you need to reduce your monthly payments in order to avoid having to file for bankruptcy. Your next step is to try to persuade your creditors to adjust your payments to fit your remaining income.

Dealing with creditors. Your next task is to create a new payment plan to present to your unsecured creditors. What you need to come up with is a plan that is fair to all of your creditors. For your unsecured creditors, you will want to reduce each payment by a proportional amount. First, take the total monthly payments of your remaining debts, and divide it by the monthly shortage. This will give you the percentage you need to reduce each debt by in order to match your remaining income.

Example: Sue has subtracted all of her essential expenses and secured loan payments from her income, and is left with $245.00. She has five monthly credit card payments as follows:

Visa	$150.00
Mastercard	65.00
Sears	50.00
Discover	23.00
Local department store	75.00
TOTAL PAYMENTS	$363.00

Sue's income is $118 short ($363 - 245 = 118). If she divides the amount she is short (118) by the total payments (363), she gets a figure of .325, which she will round up to .33 (or just about one-third). If she reduces each payment by .33 she will have enough income to meet the new payments. To find the amount to reduce each payment by, Sue will multiply each payment amount by .33, round off each answer, and then subtract this amount from each payment:

CREDITOR	OLD PAY	SUBTRACT	NEW PAY
Visa	$ 150.00	$50.00	$100.00
Mastercard	65.00	21.50	43.50
Sears	50.00	16.50	33.50
Discover	23.00	7.50	15.50
Local Dept. Store	75.00	25.00	50.00
TOTALS	363.00	120.50	242.50

As you can see, Sue has lowered her payments to fit her income, and has treated each creditor the same. If she can persuade these creditors to accept the lower payments, she has her new budget (and she has an extra $2.50 left over). Of course this will increase the number of payments needed to pay off the loans.

Once you have worked out your new proposed payment amounts it is time to contact your creditors with your plan. Letter 1 in Appendix E of this book is a form letter you can use. (see letter 1, p.207.) Space is left at the top for you to fill in the date and the name and address of the creditor. You will need to make a copy of this letter for each creditor.

Just fill in the blanks according to your new payment plan, fill in your name and address (so it can be read), sign your name and mail a copy to each creditor. Be sure to type in your name, address and account number below your signature.

NOTE: *It is a good idea to send these letters by certified, return-receipt mail. This will cost you a couple of dollars per letter, but you will later be able to prove the creditor received it if needed.*

Now sit back and wait for your creditors to answer. Be sure to fill in the return receipt number from the white receipt on both the green card and in the blank at the top of the letter. (see letter 1, p.207.) You will note that the form letter states that your next payment will be according to the new schedule unless you hear from the creditor beforehand.

You may be asking, "Why should the creditor accept reduced payments?" If the creditor really believes you are serious about bankruptcy, and sees that you have a workable budget, he has every reason to accept your plan. His alternative is to let you declare bankruptcy, in which case he will receive absolutely nothing.

You should try to get your unsecured creditors to lower their payment requirements in order to fit your budget. Only after this fails should you contact your secured creditors about a new payment schedule. You may wonder why a secured creditor would agree to lower payments, when all he has to do is repossess or foreclose. Even a secured creditor would usually rather get paid than take back the property.

It takes a lot of time and expense to repossess and resell property. If you do file for bankruptcy it will take even more time and expense. A bankruptcy will not stop foreclosure or repossession, but it will delay it. Therefore, most lenders will work with you to try to avoid foreclosure, repossession, or bankruptcy.

The key to success is showing the creditor a fair and reasonable payment plan that is clearly within your ability to maintain. If this does not work, you can still go to credit counseling, as discussed at the beginning of this section.

If this does not resolve your problem, you may need to proceed to the next section of this book to prepare for filing for bankruptcy.

Arranging Your Finances 4

> ***Warning***: *Use this section with extreme caution.* Before you file for bankruptcy, you may want to review your financial situation to see if there is anything you can rearrange to your advantage. Before we discuss various ideas, you need to be aware that you may be walking a fine line between acceptable practices and what the court might consider to be cheating your creditors. At a very minimum, you should not file for bankruptcy for at least 90 days after you make any of the changes discussed in this section, and if any changes involve a relative, you should not file for at least one year. However, each bankruptcy judge has his own ideas and attitudes, and some have determined that there was an intent to defraud where transfers were made more than a year before filing.

There are some things you might do before you file that will improve your situation after your bankruptcy is complete.

Incurring New Debts

If you will need to borrow more money to pay for necessities (such as for medical treatment, buying clothing for your family, or getting your car repaired so you can get to work), you may want to wait to file for bankruptcy until you have incurred these debts. This way, these debts can be included in your bankruptcy. A bankruptcy only affects those debts that you incur **before** you file. Any debts you incur **after** you file are not included in the bankruptcy. Just make sure you are incurring these new debts for necessary things, and not for "luxuries" (such as a vacation, a new stereo, or a night on the town).

SELLING NON-EXEMPT PROPERTY AND BUYING EXEMPT PROPERTY

The most obvious thing you might do is sell non-exempt property, and use the money to buy exempt property.

Example: If you live in New York, furniture, a radio, TV, refrigerator, and clothing are exempt. However, a boat or second car is not exempt. Therefore, you may want to sell your boat or second car, and use the money you get to buy some furniture, a radio, TV, refrigerator, or some clothing.

If you are like most people, furniture or clothing is probably your best bet, because you already have a radio, TV, and refrigerator. You will need to carefully read the list of exemptions for your state in Appendix A of this book.

SELLING NON-EXEMPT PROPERTY AND PAYING CERTAIN DEBTS

Generally, you want to sell non-exempt property, and use the money to pay off either a non-dischargeable debt (such as a student loan or overdue taxes), or pay on a secured debt on exempt property (such as catching up that overdue mortgage payment).

Example 1: You have a non-exempt boat. You sell it and use the money to pay off a student loan. In the bankruptcy you would lose the boat anyway, so you may as well use it to reduce the number of payments you'll need to make after bankruptcy on your non-dischargeable student loan.

Example 2: You have a non-exempt second car. You sell it and use the money to pay off the balance of the loan for your primary car, which is exempt in your state. You get to keep your primary car after bankruptcy, and you will have one less payment to make (provided your primary car isn't worth more than the allowable exemption).

> ***Warning:*** Be sure you do not pay off a loan on a non-exempt piece of property, because you will lose the property in bankruptcy anyway.

Example: You sell your second car and use the money to pay off your secured boat loan. The boat, being non-exempt property, is then taken by the trustee, to be sold and used to pay off other unsecured creditors. You have gained nothing.

You may also want to sell non-exempt property to pay off an unsecured loan. Paying an unsecured loan will only be of advantage under one or both of the following circumstances:

1.   A friend or relative has co-signed the loan and you do not want to stick that friend or relative with having to pay the loan for you.

2.   You want to maintain good relations with that particular creditor (such as your doctor or car repairman), and possibly be able to keep your ability to buy there on credit.

DEFRAUDING CREDITORS

Rearranging your asset and debt situation can get you into trouble. If it appears to the court that you have made changes in order to cheat your creditors, the judge can let the trustee take and sell the new property you've bought, or he can even dismiss your case and not let you have a discharge of any debts. This will leave you in a much worse situation than you began.

In order to minimize the chances of problems, keep the following points in mind:

- Do not make so many sales that you would have enough money to pay off most or all of your debts (unless this is your goal in order to avoid bankruptcy). If you sell enough property to be able to pay off your debts, and do not pay them off, it will be considered fraud.

- Sell and buy property at market value prices. If you sell something for less than reasonable or market price, or buy something for more than it is worth, your creditors may object.

- Avoid sales to, or purchases from, relatives. If you decide this is absolutely necessary, be sure you make the exchange at market value.

- Do not sell something expensive and buy something cheap, planning to secretly pocket the cash. The judge or trustee can make you account for all of the cash you get from a sale, and either you come up with the extra cash or get your case dismissed.

- If the trustee, judge, or creditors ask you about your transactions before you filed, just tell the truth. One of the main things the court will consider in deciding if your action was fraud is your intention. Furthermore, if you are asked about a particular transaction, you can be sure that the person asking the questions already knows about it. Judges do not like people who lie or are sneaky, so do not try to hide things. You are bound to get caught.

- Do not buy more non-exempt property on credit, then sell the items to buy exempt property. This is fraud.

- Do not go overboard and sell all of your non-exempt property. Leave something for the unsecured creditors so they do not feel cheated and challenge the transactions.

If all of this leaves you confused, and you want to take advantage of the things discussed in this section, you should consider consulting a lawyer.

GATHERING INFORMATION 5

Before you start preparing any forms, you will need to gather information about your finances. You should already have most, if not all, of the information you need. Your petition for bankruptcy will consist mostly of describing your financial situation at a certain point in time. You will need to gather all of your papers regarding your income, monthly expenses, assets and debts.

This information will be necessary for you to adequately fill out the forms to file for bankruptcy, and will also be useful in the event a judge, creditor or trustee asks you how you came up with the figures on your forms. The following comments regarding the type of information you need should answer any questions you have.

INCOME

For most people, income information will come from three primary sources: paystubs, tax returns, and W-2 statements. Your paystub should give the most current information. Look for a space that shows your *Year to Date*, or *YTD* income. This will give your total earnings since the beginning of the current year. You can then count the number of weeks or months that have passed since January 1st, and divide that into your year to date earnings to get an average weekly or monthly amount. If your paystub does not show a year to date figure, you can always add up the totals of all paystubs since the beginning of the year.

Another good source of income information is your previous year's income tax return, or W-2 statement. This information will be useable as long as you did not get a raise, change jobs, or have any other change in income.

If you have additional income from such things as bank account interest, stock dividends, alimony, etc., get out any statements or other records that show this income.

If you have income from self-employment, you should gather your accounting records and tax returns.

EXPENSES

You should get out any papers or records that show how much your monthly expenses are. This should include at least the following sections.

HOUSING EXPENSE

If you have a mortgage, you probably have a payment book that shows your monthly payment. If not, look for cancelled checks to the mortgage holder, a copy of the note and mortgage showing the payment, an escrow statement showing the amount withheld each month for taxes and insurance, or some similar record. If you rent, you should have a copy of a lease that shows the monthly rent, or at least cancelled checks or receipts. If you cannot find any of these, ask your mortgage company or landlord to send you a statement to verify the amount of your payment.

UTILITIES

Get out your monthly statements for your electric, gas, telephone, trash pick-up, and any other utility bill. Hopefully you have kept at least the last couple of bills. If not, be sure to keep the next one that comes. You could also write to the utility company and ask for a month-by-month statement for the past year (this information may be on some of your bills).

FOOD

This will not be as easy to find documentation for, since most people do not keep their sales receipts for food. However, if you normally write a check for your food shopping you can get an average from your checkbook information. If you cannot find any such information, you probably still have a good idea of how much you spend on food for a week or month.

LOAN PAYMENTS This information should be easy to find, in the form of a monthly statement or payment book. For credit cards you should get a monthly billing statement, which will give the balance owed and the minimum monthly payment. For other debts, such as auto loans, you will probably have a payment book.

OTHER DEBTS This includes such things as insurance premiums, gas and maintenance expenses for your car, child day care, and any other expenses. Some of these items will have some sort of documentation and some you will simply have to estimate. This information should already be on the INCOME AND EXPENSE WORKSHEET you prepared earlier. (see worksheet 1, p.159.)

PROPERTY

Next, you need to make a list of everything you own. At this point we are not concerned with how much you owe, or what it is worth. Your list will include items such as the following sections.

REAL ESTATE A deed or mortgage will sufficiently describe the property, by way of a legal description. You will probably only need the street address, but it's a good idea to have the legal description on hand.

VEHICLES You will need the year, make and model of each vehicle you own. You probably already know this information, but it is a good idea to have some paperwork on hand, such as the title, bill of sale, registration, or loan papers.

BANK ACCOUNTS, ETC. You will need copies of your most current statements, or other records, showing the current balance in all checking and savings accounts, certificates of deposit (CDs), IRA accounts, etc.

OTHER "FINANCIAL" ASSETS This includes such things as stocks and bonds, mutual funds, annuities, life insurance policies with a cash value, and any kind of retirement account or fund. All of these things should have some kind of statement or other paperwork to show current values.

JEWELRY AND OTHER COLLECTIBLES
These items will probably not have any papers to document their value, unless you have had the item appraised or insured for a certain amount, or have borrowed money to buy the item. (Unless you still happen to have the receipt for an item that has not gone up in value much since you bought it.) When there is no documentation, make a list of the items and estimate what you could sell it for.

OTHER PERSONAL BELONGINGS
This category includes all of your furniture, clothing, pots, pans and dishes, and other everyday personal possessions. Of course, if any of these items are especially valuable, you need to treat them the same as jewelry and collectibles. Otherwise, just make a note in each category with an amount you think it would cost to replace the entire category. It is not necessary for you to list each piece of clothing, or each pot and pan, separately.

DEBTS

The most common debts are a mortgage, auto loan, and credit cards. A debt will have an outstanding balance, and almost certainly an interest rate. This distinguishes a debt from other monthly obligations such as rent and utility payments. There will also be either a monthly statement or payment book, and probably some other paperwork you completed or received when you first obtained the credit. Mainly, you will need to know the name and address of whom the money is owed to, the account number, and the amount owed.

LEGAL RESEARCH

As the law is subject to change at any time, it is strongly suggested that you review your state's exemption laws before you file. The best place to do this is at a law library, and the best place to find such a library is at your local courthouse. Law schools also have good law libraries.

There are two main sources of information:

1. your state's laws, which are in your state's exemptions in Appendix A of this book and

2. the *Bankruptcy Reporter*, which is a nationwide collection of the decisions of the various bankruptcy courts.

If you find an annotated set of laws for your state, they will also refer to significant court decisions.

STATE LAWS

State laws are most often referred to as *statutes* or *codes*, and contain the exact law as passed by your state legislature. The laws are identified by numbers called *titles*, *chapters*, or *sections*, depending upon your state's system. A few states (namely Maryland, New York, and Texas) break the laws down by subject first, then break each subject down into sections. Once you find the particular law relating to your exemption, read the exact language to be sure there aren't any special qualifications required for the exemption.

Supplement. In addition to the main volume, there is another place you should look. All of the states periodically update their statutes. Some states do this by a paperback supplement that slides into a pocket in the back of the hard-cover volume. Other states publish a separate hard-cover or paperback volume, which you can find as the last book of the series of laws. A few states have their statutes in loose-leaf binders, with separate supplement sections. Be sure to check the supplement.

Annotation. Many states also have sets of laws that are *annotated*. This means that, after each law is stated, there is more information to help you understand what the law means. This includes brief summaries of court decisions interpreting that law. The supplements will also be annotated, which is where you will find the most recent information.

BANKRUPTCY REPORTER

The *Bankruptcy Reporter* is a multi-volume set of books containing court decisions in bankruptcy cases. In most cases, you will only be concerned with the more recent, paperback volumes. The index in the front of each volume contains a summary of the court decisions. Look for decisions from your state, which is abbreviated at the beginning of each summary.

PRACTICE
MANUALS

If you really want to study the details of bankruptcy law, look for a practice manual on bankruptcy. A practice manual is a book, or set of books, that gives detailed information on a specific area of law. A leading practice manual in the field of bankruptcy law is *Collier Bankruptcy Manual*, published by Matthew Bender, along with its companion *Collier Forms Manual*. Your law library will probably have a section devoted to such bankruptcy books. These books will contain additional forms, as well as detailed information on all aspects of bankruptcy law.

If you have any difficulty, ask the librarian for assistance. However, do not expect the librarian to give you any legal advice.

INTERNET
SOURCES

There are several sources of bankruptcy information and forms on the Internet. These include:

- Findlaw, which offers information on just about any legal topic and includes links to the text of federal and state laws. To go directly to bankruptcy information and forms:

  http://www.findlaw.com/01topics/03bankruptcy/index.html

  http://guide.lp.findlaw.com/10fedgov/judicial/bankruptcy-courts.html

  http://forms.lp.findlaw.com/federal/fjnbf_1.html

- The text of the Bankruptcy Code can also be found at:

  http://www4.law.cornell.edu/uscode/11/

- InterNet Bankruptcy Library:

  http://bankrupt.com/

- ABI World (American Bankruptcy Institute):

  http:www.abiworld.org/

- Bankruptcy Alternatives:

  http://www.berkshire.net/~mkb/

COURT FORMS 6

This section will help you to use and understand the legal forms that you prepare. These forms are found in Appendix D of this book. Make copies of the forms you need, and save the originals from the book in case you make a mistake or need to make changes.

You will not need every form found in Appendix D, as some of them will not apply to your situation. Certain forms apply only to Chapter 7 bankruptcies; certain forms apply only to Chapter 13 bankruptcies; and others can be used with either type of case. By now you should have decided upon whether you will file a Chapter 7 or a Chapter 13 case, so just follow the instructions in the next section of this book.

UNDERSTANDING LEGAL FORMS

Legal forms are simply means of communicating necessary information to the court. Forms serve two main functions. First, they ask the court to do something (such as give you a discharge of your debts). Second, they provide the court with the information it needs to decide whether to give you what you ask for.

The following sections of this book will tell you how to fill in each specific form. We will discuss how to fill in the top portion of the forms here. You will notice that some of the forms begin as follows:

UNITED STATES BANKRUPTCY COURT
_____ DISTRICT OF _____

This is to show which court you are filing your papers with. Anyone who looks at your papers later will be able to know which court to go to in order to find more details about your bankruptcy case. Your creditors may need this information during the bankruptcy case. Also, after your case is completed, and you are applying for a mortgage or car loan, your prospective lender may need this information.

Each state has both state and federal courts. The first line tells you that this case is in the federal district bankruptcy court. Each state has at least one federal district bankruptcy court, and most have two or more. States that are divided into two districts will be divided one of the two following ways:

1.   Eastern District and Western District.

2.   Northern District and Southern District.

States that are divided into three districts will also be divided one of the two ways listed above, but will also have a Middle District. To find out which district you live in (and will file your case in), look in your phone directory for the number of the U.S. District Court or U.S. Bankruptcy Court. This should be listed in the government section of your phone directory. Call the court and ask which district covers your area.

The district designation will need to be typed in the first space on each form you use. If you live in a state with only one district, leave this space blank. The name of your state needs to be typed in the second space. For example, if you live in Florida, and you are in the Southern District, your forms will look like this when completed:

UNITED STATES BANKRUPTCY COURT

Southern   DISTRICT OF _____ Florida _____

You may want to make a trip to your bankruptcy court clerk's office and ask to see a Chapter 7 or Chapter 13 case that someone else has filed. This may help you in completing your forms. The court records are open to the public, although you will not be allowed to take the case file out of the clerk's office. There will probably be an area at the clerk's office where you can sit down and review a file.

The next part of the form looks like this:

In re _____   Case No._____

NOTE: *The VOLUNTARY PETITION, which has its own instructions on page 52, does not have the above as the next part of the form. (see form 1, p.165.)*

In the space after "In re," you will type in your name, as well as your spouse's name if you are married and filing together. The "Case No." will be left blank on your VOLUNTARY PETITION, because the court clerk will assign your case a number and fill it in this space when you file. Then, you will type in the case number on any papers you file later.

The forms in this book follow those approved by the bankruptcy courts throughout the country. The bankruptcy rules require all of the bankruptcy courts to accept these forms.

It is not absolutely necessary that you use a typewriter to fill in the forms, although typing is preferred by the court and gives a much more professional appearance than handwriting. If typing is not possible, then *print* the information and be sure that your writing can be easily read. The remainder of each form will be discussed in detail in the following section of this book. Just remember to complete the top part of each form.

Also note that many of the forms have two shaded circles at the top. The bankruptcy rules require all papers filed with the court clerk to be hole-punched so the clerk can insert them in a file folder. Get a paper punch and punch out the shaded circles.

The following subsections will give you detailed instructions for filling out the necessary bankruptcy court forms. (worksheets 1 through 3 are the worksheets you completed in Section 6 of this book. The forms in Appendix D are the forms that you may need to file with the court.) Most of the forms are the same regardless of whether you have decided to file under Chapter 7 or under Chapter 13 of the Bankruptcy Code. For both Chapters you will file the following forms:

- **VOLUNTARY PETITION** (form 1)

- **SUMMARY OF SCHEDULES** (form 3)

- **SCHEDULES A** through **J** (form 4 through form 13)

- **DECLARATION CONCERNING DEBTOR'S SCHEDULES** (form 14)

- **STATEMENT OF FINANCIAL AFFAIRS** (form 15)

If you are filing under Chapter 7 you will also file a **CHAPTER 7 INDIVIDUAL DEBTOR'S STATEMENT OF INTENTION**. (see form 16, p.198.) If you are filing under Chapter 13 you will file a **CHAPTER 13 PLAN**. (see form 17, p.199.)

The following instructions relate to the form number, which is located in the upper outside corner of the first page of each form. Some of the forms are more than one page, and several have continuation pages for use if there is not enough room on the first page.

VOLUNTARY PETITION (form 1)

To complete the **VOLUNTARY PETITION** (see form 1, p.165):

- First, fill in the designation of the bankruptcy court in which you will be filing your case.

- Next fill in the names, addresses, and social security number (or numbers if you and your spouse are filing a joint petition) in the boxes as indicated.

- Under the heading "INFORMATION REGARDING THE DEBTOR," check the appropriate box or boxes.

- Under the heading "VENUE" check the first box. (The second box is for businesses. If you have an affiliate, general partner, or partnership, you should consult a lawyer, or a business bankruptcy book.)

☛ Under "TYPE OF DEBTOR" check the box for "Individual(s)."

☛ Under "NATURE OF DEBT" check "Consumer/Non-Business." Ignore the section titled "Chapter 11 Small Business."

☛ Under "CHAPTER OR SECTION OF BANKRUPTCY CODE UNDER WHICH THE PETITION IS FILED" check either the box for "Chapter 7" or for "Chapter 13," whichever one you have decided to use.

☛ Under "FILING FEE" check whichever box applies to your situation.

☛ Under the section titled "STATISTICAL ADMINISTRATIVE INFORMATION," check the boxes that reflect your situation. This information can be determined from the information on worksheets 1, 2, and 3 that you have completed.

☛ At the top of the second page of the VOLUNTARY PETITION, type in your name (and your spouse's name if you are filing a joint petition). If you have filed for bankruptcy within the past six years, or if your spouse has filed a bankruptcy case that is currently pending, you will need to fill in the information where indicated.

☛ Next, in the section designated "SIGNATURE(S) OF DEBTOR(S) (INDIVIDUAL/JOINT)," sign your name and fill in your phone number and the date on the lines where indicated. If you and your spouse are filing a joint petition, your spouse must sign also. Ignore the other sections.

NOTE: *In Appendix D there is the* SUMMARY OF SCHEDULES. *(see form 3, p.169.) Skip this form for now. It will be completed after you complete Schedules A through J.*

APPLICATION TO PAY FILING FEE IN INSTALLMENTS (form 2)

Use the APPLICATION TO PAY FILING FEE IN INSTALLMENTS (see form 2, p.167) if you are unable to pay the full filing fees at the time you file your VOLUNTARY PETITION. If you *are* able to pay the full filing fee when you file your VOLUNTARY PETITION, you can ignore form 2.

Call the court clerk's office to confirm the amount of the filing fee. You can expect it to run about $200 for a Chapter 7 case, and about $185 for a Chapter 13 case. You may pay the filing fee in installments, provided that there are no more than four installments and that the last payment is made no later than 120 days after the VOLUNTARY PETITION is filed. Fees can also be found on various bankruptcy court websites and at 28 U.S.C. §1930.

☞ Complete the top portion of the form according to the instructions in "Understanding Legal Forms" at the beginning of this section on page 49.

☞ Then, fill in the amount of the filing fee on the line in paragraph 1.

☞ In paragraph 4, fill in the installment payment terms on the lines provided.

☞ Next, sign your name on the appropriate line (and have your spouse sign if you are filing a joint petition), and fill in the date. Ignore the other items on the first page of this form.

☞ The second page of this form is the order the judge will sign to give you permission to pay in installments. All you need to do here is fill in the designation of the court at the top of the page.

☞ Fill in your name on the line marked "Debtor" (and your spouse's name if filing jointly).

☞ Fill in the chapter of the bankruptcy code (7 or 13).

The court clerk will fill in the case number and the judge will complete the remainder of the page.

If you do not think you can pay the fees in installments, ask the court clerk if there are any provisions or forms for having the fees waived entirely. If not, you may want to contact a legal aid office in your area.

SCHEDULE A—REAL PROPERTY (form 4)

SCHEDULE A—REAL PROPERTY is where you will list all real estate you own. (see form 4, p.170.) First of all, be sure to carefully read the instructions contained at the top of the form itself. This is the form where you list all of the real estate you own or have an interest in. In general, *real property* means land and things permanently attached to it (like a house).

☞ If you do not have an interest in any real property, simply write "None" in the first column that is headed "DESCRIPTION AND LOCATION OF PROPERTY." If you do have an interest in real property, you will need to complete the rest of this form.

☞ In the first column, you will describe the property and tell where it is located. This does not have to be the formal legal description, but you should state the type of property (such as "home," "unimproved lot," "condominium," etc.), and the address, including the city, county and state. If you are renting the property, it should not be listed on this form, but should be listed on SCHEDULE G - EXECUTORY CONTRACTS AND UNEXPIRED LEASES instead. (see form 10, p.182.)

☞ In the second column, designated "NATURE OF DEBTOR'S INTEREST IN PROPERTY," state the type of interest you have in the property. For most people who own a home, the ownership interest in the property is known as *fee simple*. The most common interests in real property are as follows:

- *Fee Simple*: This is where you own the property, with no obligation other than to pay the mortgage and taxes. You may own the property with someone else or by yourself.

- *Life Estate*: This is where you have the right to live in the property during your lifetime, but you can't sell or give it away during your lifetime, or leave it to anyone upon your death. This is commonly set up when the husband dies, and is usually done for tax purposes. He gives his widow a life estate so that she can live in the property until she dies, but then the property goes to their children.

- *Future Interest*: The most common example of this kind of interest is what the children have after a life estate for their mother. A person with a future interest will get the property someday, but only after some event occurs (such as the death of the person with the life estate).

One of these types of interests should be listed in the second column. If you own the property with another person who is not your husband or wife, you should also indicate the portion of the interest you own (such as *one-half fee simple*, or *one-third future interest*).

☞ If you are not married, you may ignore the third column. If you are married, you need to indicate whether each piece of property is owned by the husband (H), the wife (W), both of you jointly (J), or both of you as *community property* (C).

NOTE: *Community property only applies if you live in Arizona, California, Idaho, Louisiana, Nevada, New Mexico, Texas, Washington, or Wisconsin. Generally, this means that all the property either spouse obtains during the marriage is owned by both of them, and can be taken by the trustee even if they don't file for bankruptcy jointly. If you live in one of these states and are considering filing separately from your spouse, you should consult a bankruptcy lawyer.*

☞ In the fourth column, indicate the market value of the property. This is what the property could most likely be sold for. **Do not** take into account any money you owe on the mortgage. Be sure to total these amounts at the bottom of this column.

● In the fifth column, indicate the amount of money you owe on the mortgage or any liens on the property. If you do not owe any money on the property, write "None" in the fifth column.

SCHEDULE B—PERSONAL PROPERTY (form 5)

On SCHEDULE B—PERSONAL PROPERTY, you will list all of your property that is *not* real estate. (see form 5, p.171.) Be sure to carefully read the instructions on the form itself. Also note that this form is several pages long. *Personal property* is all of your property that is *not* land or permanently attached to the land. This will be everything you listed in the PROPERTY WORKSHEET, except for the real estate items. (see worksheet 2, p.160.)

● The types of personal property are listed in the first column of this form. Simply read each item and write down what you own in that category.

● If you do not own anything in a particular category, simply check the second column marked "NONE."

> *Warning*: Be sure to list all of your property, even if you think it has no value. Otherwise, it may appear you are trying to hide property from creditors, which could result in the dismissal of your case.

● In the third column, marked "DESCRIPTION AND LOCATION OF PROPERTY," describe each item in the category, and indicate where it is located by street address, city, county and state. If most of the property is at your home, you may write in "Unless otherwise indicated, all property is located at the debtor's residence." If you do this, be sure to indicate any property that is located somewhere else.

Refer to Appendix A of this book for the list of the exemptions for your state, and for the alternate Federal Bankruptcy Exemptions. Any item for which you may claim an exemption should be listed separately in this form.

Example: Item 11 relates to pension plans. If your state offers an exemption for a certain type of plan, be sure to indicate that your plan is of that type. (See Section 8, page 85 of this book regarding pension plans.)

☛ If you are not married you may ignore the fourth column. If you are married, you will need to indicate whether the property is owned by the husband (H), the wife (W), both of you jointly (J), or both of you as community property (C).

☛ In the last column, indicate the market value of the property. Unless you know what the property is worth, you should use your best guess as to what it would sell for at a garage sale. You want to estimate on the low side, but don't get ridiculous or you may get challenged by the trustee or a creditor.

☛ Total the amounts in this column at the bottom of the third page of the form.

SCHEDULE C—PROPERTY CLAIMED AS EXEMPT (form 6)

The property you are claiming as exempt from your creditors must be listed in SCHEDULE C—PROPERTY CLAIMED AS EXEMPT. (see form 6, p.174.)

☛ First you need to check one of the boxes at the top, indicating whether you are using the Federal Bankruptcy Exemptions (the first box), or the exemptions for your state (the second box). Both types of federal exemptions, and your state's exemptions are found in Appendix A of this book. The Federal Bankruptcy Exemptions are only available in certain states, which are listed under the federal exemptions in Appendix A.

NOTE: *If the Federal Bankruptcy Exemptions are available in your state, you need to compare them with those of your state to see which set will allow you to keep more of your property. If you select the state exemptions, you may also use the Federal Non-Bankruptcy Exemptions.*

☞ To complete the rest of SCHEDULE C—PROPERTY CLAIMED AS EXEMPT (form 6), refer to Column (5) of the PROPERTY WORKSHEET, where you have already identified the items you are claiming as exempt. (see worksheet 2, p.160.) You may want to refer once again to the information in Appendix A of this book to be sure you are claiming everything to which you may be entitled.

If you are not sure whether you can claim an item, but it seems to fit one of the exemptions, then claim it! Let the trustee or a creditor question it. (Of course, do not claim something you know is not exempt, but if you genuinely are not sure give yourself the benefit of the exemption.)

☞ In the first column, write in a description of the property. Try to use the same categories as those for your state in Appendix A.

NOTE: *All of the property listed in this form should also be listed in either SCHEDULE A—REAL PROPERTY (form 4) or in SCHEDULE B—PERSONAL PROPERTY (form 5).*

☞ In the second column, indicate the statute or law that gives you the exemption you are claiming. Again, refer to Appendix A of this book for the statute or law number. Examples of how to refer to these laws appear at the beginning of each state's listing in Appendix A.

☞ In the third column, marked "VALUE OF CLAIMED EXEMPTION," state the amount of the exemption you are claiming. Be sure you are not exceeding the maximum amount of the exemption allowed as indicated in Appendix A.

Example: If your state only allows up to a $2,000 exemption for a car, don't show a $30,000 exemption for your Mercedes.

☞ In the last column indicate the full market value of the property.

SCHEDULE D—CREDITORS HOLDING SECURED CLAIMS (form 7)

Any secured creditors need to be listed on SCHEDULE D—CREDITORS HOLDING SECURED CLAIMS. (see form 7, p.175.) Be sure to carefully read the instructions at the beginning of the form itself. To complete this form refer to the DEBT WORKSHEET, Column (4), which will show those creditors holding a security interest in your property. (see worksheet 3, p.161.) These will most likely be the mortgage on your home and any other real property, and the lenders on auto, boat or home improvement loans. (They are not likely to be credit card companies.)

A creditor holding security is one who loaned you money to buy something, and has the right to take some of your property if you don't pay. This also includes anyone having a lien on your property, such as for work done on your home.

- In the first column indicate the account number (if any), and the creditor's name and address.

- Place an "X" in the second column, marked "CODEBTOR," if another person is also liable for the repayment of the debt. However, do not check this column if the other person is your spouse *and* you and your spouse have filed a joint bankruptcy petition.

- If you are not married, ignore the third column. If you are married, then indicate here whether the debt is owed by the husband (H), the wife (W), both of you jointly (J), or both of you as a community property debt (C).

- In the fourth column, first indicate the date the debt was created. Next, indicate the nature of the lien on the property. Refer to the first paragraph of instructions on the form itself for examples of the types of liens. If you aren't sure of the type of lien, simply write "nature uncertain" and ask the trustee later; or call the person or company you owe the money to and ask. Next, give a description of the property that is subject to the lien, and indicate the full value of the property in the space labeled "VALUE $."

☞ In the fifth, sixth, and seventh columns, indicate (by an "X") if the debt is *contingent, unliquidated,* or *disputed*. These concepts are very confusing, so do not hesitate to ask the trustee if you are not sure.

A contingent debt is one that will only be owed if some future event occurs (such as if a tax audit shows that a debt claimed by IRS is really owed).

An unliquidated debt is one in which the exact amount hasn't been determined (such as where you know you owe a tax, but won't know the exact amount until you know the full amount of your income or expenses).

A disputed debt is one you are contesting (someone is claiming you owe the debt, but you don't think you do or don't think you owe as much).

If none of these apply, leave these columns blank.

☞ In the eighth column, marked "AMOUNT OF CLAIM WITH-OUT DEDUCTING VALUE OF COLLATERAL," indicate the amount of the debt you owe.

☞ In the last column, indicate if any of the debt is *unsecured* (not attached to any piece of property).

Example: If you owe $8,000 on your car, but the car is only worth $6,000, then $2,000 of the debt is unsecured.

☞ Total the eighth column, and indicate at the bottom left if there are any continuation sheets attached.

NOTE: *There is a continuation sheet for this form. Indicate at the bottom left whether there are any continuation sheets attached.*

☞ If you only use the first page, total the eighth column and type in the amount in the box marked "Total."

☞ If you use one of more continuation pages, total the eighth column for each page and type the amount in the box marked "Subtotal." Then add all of the subtotals and type the amount in the box marked "Total" on the last page.

SCHEDULE E—CREDITORS HOLDING UNSECURED PRIORITY CLAIMS (form 8)

Certain types of creditors have *priority*, which means that they will be paid from your non-exempt and non-secured property before other creditors. Most creditors with priority relate to the operation of a business, so they will not apply to most people filing for personal bankruptcy under Chapter 7 or 13. The priority claims are listed on SCHEDULE E—CREDITORS HOLDING UNSECURED PRIORITY CLAIMS. (see form 8, p.177.) They are as follows:

- *extensions of credit in an involuntary case*. Since you are filing a voluntary petition, this does not apply to you.

- *wages, salaries and commissions*. This relates to money that you would owe to your employee. If you have employees, you should either consult an attorney or a book that deals with business bankruptcy.

- *contributions to employee benefit plans*. Again, if you have employees, you should consult a lawyer or a book dealing with business bankruptcy.

- *certain farmers and fishermen*. This only applies to operators of grain or fish storage facilities.

● *deposits by individuals.* This would apply to you only if you owe someone money for a deposit they gave you to purchase or rent real estate, goods, or services that you have not provided.

● *taxes and certain other debts owed to the government.* If you owe taxes to the federal, state, or local government, you will need to check this box and list the debt.

● *alimony, maintenance or support.* This applies if you owe court-ordered alimony, maintenance, or support to a former spouse or a child.

● *commitments to maintain the capital of an insured depository institution.* This only applies to banks or other similar depository institutions.

Be sure to carefully read the instructions at the beginning of form 8.

☛ If you do not have any of these types of debts, check the first box on the first page of form 8 that states: "Check this box if the debtor has no creditors holding unsecured priority claims to report on this Schedule E."

☛ If you do have any of these types of debts, then check the appropriate box or boxes on the first page, and list the debt on the continuation sheet. Complete a separate continuation sheet for each type of debt listed.

NOTE: *There is a space at the top of the continuation sheet for indicating the type of priority debt.*

☛ To complete the remainder of the continuation sheet, follow the same directions for the SCHEDULE D—CREDITORS HOLDING SECURED CLAIMS given on page 60. Be sure to total the amounts in the eighth column, and indicate at the bottom left how many continuations sheets are provided for SCHEDULE E.

SCHEDULE F—CREDITORS HOLDING UNSECURED NONPRIORITY CLAIMS (form 9)

All of the creditors not listed on any of the previous forms will be listed on SCHEDULE F—CREDITORS HOLDING UNSECURED NONPRIORITY CLAIMS. (see form 9, p.180.) In most cases this will be primarily credit cards, and other personal debts such as unpaid bills. Be sure to carefully read the instructions at the beginning of the form itself. This form also has a continuation sheet.

NOTE: *There is a box to check if you have no creditors to report on this form. If you have no creditors to report here, you need to go back to Section 3 of this book and take another look at whether you can, or should, avoid bankruptcy.*

The main benefit of bankruptcy is getting rid of these unsecured nonpriority claims. If you have none to get rid of, you probably should not file for bankruptcy and may want to consult a lawyer or credit counselor.

☞ Complete the first, second, and third columns according to the instructions for SCHEDULE D—CREDITORS HOLDING SECURED CLAIMS, as indicated on page 60.

☞ In the fourth column, indicate the date the claim was incurred, the consideration for the claim, and any setoff you are claiming.

For the "consideration," simply state what the debt was for, such as "student loan," "vacation loan," "dental bill," "car repair," "Visa," "Sears," etc.

In some cases, a store may have required you to pledge some property as collateral in order to obtain the credit card. You should know if this is the case because you probably would have had to sign some additional papers instead of a simple credit card application.

If this is the case with one of your credit cards, you should list it on SCHEDULE D instead of here. (see form 7, p.175.)

A *setoff* is a debt the creditor owes to you.

Example: If you owe your landlord $800 in back rent, but he owes you $50 for plumbing repairs that you paid for, you have an setoff of $50.

☛ Complete the remaining columns according to the instructions for the same columns in SCHEDULE D, as indicated on page 60-62.

☛ This form also has a continuation sheet, so be sure to indicate at the bottom the number of continuation sheets attached.

☛ Total the amounts in the last column.

SCHEDULE G—EXECUTORY CONTRACTS AND UNEXPIRED LEASES (form 10)

Any contracts or leases to which you are a party must be listed and described on SCHEDULE G—EXECUTORY CONTRACTS AND UNEXPIRED LEASES. (see form 10, p.182.)

☛ If you are not a party to any contracts or leases, simply check the box near the top of the form before the sentence "Check this box if debtor has no executory contracts or unexpired leases." Be sure to carefully read the instructions at the beginning of the form itself.

☛ In the first column, indicate the name and address of the other parties to the contract or lease. This includes anyone who is obligated the same as you, such as your apartment roommate if his or her name is also on the lease. It also includes the person to whom you are obligated, such as your landlord.

☛ In the second column, describe the contract or lease. Examples of such descriptions are "apartment lease," "auto lease," "lawn maintenance contract," etc. In this column you must also list the nature of your interest, such as "lessee," "seller," or "purchaser." (If you are a landlord, you will state this as "lessor.") If you have a lease for nonresidential property, you need to indicate this; and if you are a party to a government contract, the contract number must be stated.

SCHEDULE H—CODEBTORS (form 11)

Anyone who is also obligated to pay all or part of any of your debts must be listed on SCHEDULE H—CODEBTORS. (see form 11, p.183.) You do not need to include your spouse if you are filing a joint bankruptcy petition. Be sure to carefully read the instructions at the beginning of the form itself.

NOTE: *There is a box to check if you have no codebtors. If you do have any codebtors, then indicate their name and address in the first column, and the creditor's name and address in the second column.*

SCHEDULE I—CURRENT INCOME OF INDIVIDUAL DEBTOR(S) (form 12)

SCHEDULE I—CURRENT INCOME OF INDIVIDUAL DEBTOR(S) is where you list your income, and that of your spouse if you are married and are filing a joint petition for bankruptcy. (see form 12, p.184.) You will also need to fill in your spouse's income if you are filing under Chapter 13, even if you are not filing a joint petition.

The top portion of this form asks form information about your family status and employment, and is self-explanatory. The lower part asks for a breakdown of your income and payroll deductions (and that of your spouse if you are married and filing a joint petition, or are married and filing under Chapter 13). All amounts should be converted to a monthly amount. The last sentence in the form asks you to describe any increase or decrease of more than 10% in any of the listed categories that you expect to occur within the year after filing the petition. Examples would be the termination of unemployment benefits, an anticipated layoff or wage reduction, or the loss of rental income from the imminent sale of the property.

SCHEDULE J—CURRENT EXPENDITURES OF INDIVIDUAL DEBTOR(S) (form 13)

The previous schedule listed your income. SCHEDULE J—CURRENT EXPENDITURES OF INDIVIDUAL DEBTOR(S) is to list your monthly expenses. (see form 13, p.185.) Convert all amounts to monthly figures. If you and your spouse are filing a joint petition, but do not live together, you will need to check the box near the top of the form, and your spouse will also need to complete a separate SCHEDULE J (in which case you will need to make another copy of this form for your spouse to complete).

NOTE: *At the bottom of this form there is a section to be completed* **only** *if you are filing under Chapter 13 of the Bankruptcy Code.*

☛ In item "A" use the total income figure from form 12.

☛ In item "B" use the "TOTAL MONTHLY EXPENSES" from this form.

☛ Item "C" will give the total amount you have available to pay your creditors under your Chapter 13 Plan.

☛ If you are going to pay monthly, indicate "month" in item "D."

☛ If you are going to pay at some other interval, you will need to divide the figure in "C" by the appropriate number to indicate how much you will pay at each interval chosen.

SUMMARY OF SCHEDULES (form 3)

On the SUMMARY OF SCHEDULES you will give the totals from each of the schedules you have completed. (see form 3, p.169.)

NOTE: *For each schedule you are to indicate the number of sheets used. You will need to count the number of continuation sheets for each schedule, and don't forget to count your spouse's separate SCHEDULE J—CURRENT EXPENDITURES OF INDIVIDUAL DEBTOR(S) if appropriate. (see form 13, p.185.)*

Be sure to add the totals of the columns where indicated. Do not leave any spaces blank. If there is no entry for an item, type "0" in the space for that item. Although you are completing this form after the other schedules, this form will come before the other schedules when you file your petition.

DECLARATION CONCERNING DEBTOR'S SCHEDULES (form 14)

By completing and signing the DECLARATION CONCERNING DEBTOR'S SCHEDULES you swear that your schedules are accurate to the best of your knowledge. (see form 14, p.186.) To complete this form:

☞ Type in the total number of sheets as indicated on the form.

☞ Type in the date.

☞ Sign your name where indicated (your spouse must also do the same if you are filing jointly).

   NOTE: *There are a fine and jail penalties listed on the form for giving false information.*

☞ Ignore the sections titled "Certification and Signature of Non-Attorney Bankruptcy Petition Preparer" and "Declaration Under Penalty of Perjury on Behalf of a Corporation or Partnership."

STATEMENT OF FINANCIAL AFFAIRS (form 15)

The STATEMENT OF FINANCIAL AFFAIRS is a lengthy form, but one that is not difficult to complete because the instructions on the form itself are rather clear. (see form 15, p.187.) All you need to do is read each item and provide the information it asks for. For each item there is a box marked "None" to check if that item does not apply to you. Be sure you mark the "None" box instead of leaving an item unanswered.

Some of the questions may require you to go back through your records for the past few years. Just answer the questions as best you can with the information you can recall or locate. Use additional sheets of paper if necessary, and be sure to indicate the number of the item being continued on the additional sheet.

Item 19 asks about property you have that belongs to someone else. This is to protect that person's property from your creditors. Of course, an easier way to deal with this situation is for you to return that property to the other person.

Read the instructions immediately before Item 19 carefully. You will not need to complete any more of the numbered items in this form (and can skip to the last page for your signature) unless you have been in one of the following positions within the past two years:

- an officer, director, or managing executive of a corporation;

- an owner of more than 5% of the voting stock of a corporation;

- a general partner in a partnership; or

- a sole proprietor of a business, or otherwise self-employed.

Once you have completed all of the items you are required to complete, type in the date and sign your name where indicated on the last page of the STATEMENT OF FINANCIAL AFFAIRS. Your spouse must also date and sign this form if you are filing a joint petition. Also, indicate the number of continuation sheets attached (type in "0" if there are none).

NOTE: *There are a fine and jail penalties listed at the end of the form for giving false information.*

Chapter 7 Individual Debtor's Statement of Intention (form 16)

If you are filing under Chapter 13 of the Bankruptcy Code, ignore this section and go on to the section about the **Chapter 13 Plan.** (see form 17, p.199.) If you are filing under Chapter 7 you will need to complete the **Chapter 7 Individual Debtor's Statement of Intention.** (see form 16, p.198.) This simply indicates what secured property you intend to give up to your creditors and which property you intend to keep. This form only applies to *secured* property.

To complete form 16:

- ☛ Complete the caption according to the instructions at the beginning of this Section.

- ☛ Under the part of this form designated "a. Property to Be Surrendered," you will list the secured property you are giving up to be used to pay creditors. In the first column, describe the property being given up in sufficient detail so that it is clear what is being forfeited.

    Example: If you are giving up one car and keeping another, it would not be sufficient to simply state "automobile." In the second column, fill in the name of the creditor who will get that item of property. This will be the creditor holding the mortgage, lien, or financing statement on that property.

    You may keep secured property by informally agreeing with the creditor that they will not foreclose or repossess as long as you maintain agreed upon payments. If you are current in your payments, you can probably keep the property by simply continuing your regular payments. This is the preferable situation. If you are going to proceed with such an informal arrangement, you will still list the property under this part of the form. This is because you are formally surrendering your rights under the Bankruptcy Code to redeem the property or reaffirm the debt.

☞ Under the part of this form designated "b. Property to Be Retained," you will list secured property you intend to keep. In order to list an item under this part, you must either claim the property as exempt, redeem the property, or reaffirm the debt. Read the paragraph following these instructions, see Section 8 of this book for detailed information on redeeming property and reaffirming debts, then see a lawyer if you think you want to redeem property or reaffirm a debt.

☞ Fill in the date where indicated, and sign your name on the line marked "Signature of Debtor." Ignore the section of this form marked "Certification of Non-Attorney Bankruptcy Petition Preparer."

There can be many complications to redeeming property or reaffirming a debt. Be sure to read more about these subjects in Section 8 of this book. It is the common practice of many creditors to attempt to talk the debtor into reaffirming the debt, often to the debtor's detriment. If you run into a situation where you are not certain that your creditor will not foreclose or repossess, and will allow you to continue payments, you should see a lawyer.

Date and sign the form on the lines indicated. This form is very poorly designed, however, it is the official form approved by the bankruptcy courts. Ignore the section titled "Certification of Non-Attorney Bankruptcy Petition Preparer."

CHAPTER 13 PLAN (form 17)

If you are filing under Chapter 7 of the Bankruptcy Code, you should ignore this form. If you are filing under Chapter 13 you will need to complete the CHAPTER 13 PLAN, which simply states how you intend to pay your creditor from your disposable income. (see form 17, p.199.) At the bottom of SCHEDULE J—CURRENT EXPENDITURES OF INDIVIDUAL DEBTOR(S), you will find your disposable, or *excess* income. (see form 13, p.185.) This is the amount of money you have available to turn over to the trustee in order to pay your debts. The following instructions will help you complete your CHAPTER 13 PLAN.

☞ In the paragraph before numbered paragraph 1, type in the amount and indicate the payment interval from the bottom of SCHEDULE J—CURRENT EXPENDITURES OF INDIVIDUAL DEBTORS. (see form 13, p.185.) In deciding the interval to use, you may want to make it the same as your paycheck schedule.

☞ In the paragraph numbered 2, describe how you want to pay your secured debts.

NOTE: *If you do not pay secured debts the lender can repossess the property. Therefore, you will want to keep up the full payments on these debts.*

List the name of the lender, the amount of the debt, and the periodic payment to be made.

☞ In the paragraph numbered 3, describe how you want to pay your unsecured debts.

• Deduct the total amount of your payments on your secured debts from your disposable income. This will give you how much is left to pay your unsecured creditors. Generally, you must pay each unsecured creditor the same percentage of the debt as the other unsecured creditors. This may be done over a period of up to three years.

If you have enough income to pay all of these debts in full within three years, you will set up a schedule to accomplish this by dividing the amount owed to each creditor by 36 months. This will give you the amount to pay to each creditor each month.

If you do not have enough income to pay all of your debts in full within three years, the following paragraph will help you determine how much you can pay.

- To determine how much debt you can pay, use the following steps:

  1. Take your monthly disposable income, subtract the total monthly payments to secured creditors, and multiply the answer by 36. This will give you the total amount you have available to pay over the three years.

  2. Add total amount you owe to all of your unsecured creditors.

  3. Divide the total from "2" above by the total in "1." This will give you the percentage of each debt you will be able to pay.

  4. For each debt, multiply the total amount owed by the answer from "3."

  5. Take the answer from "4" and divide it by 36. This will give you how much of your monthly disposable income should be applied to each debt. Convert this to match your pay period if necessary (such as to a weekly or semi-monthly amount).

  In paragraph 3 of your **CHAPTER 13 PLAN** (form 17), type in the name of each creditor, the amount to be paid each month, and percentage of the amount due that will be paid (from "3" above).

- Paragraph 5 contains a box to check if there is an addendum to the form. This will be used if you need additional space, or if there are any special arrangements regarding the payment of your debts.

- Date and sign the form. This form should be filed along with your petition, and ***must*** be filed no more than 15 days after filing your petition.

MASTER ADDRESS LISTS AND MAILING MATRIX (form 18)

All bankruptcy courts require the debtor to provide information on creditors so that the court clerk can mail the required notices to the creditors. You need to check with the bankruptcy court clerk where you will be filing your case to determine the requirements you will need to meet. Some courts have their requirements set forth online. To find out if your court has online information, go to:

http://guide.lp.findlaw.com/10fedgov/judicial/bankruptcy-courts.html

You can then scroll down to see if your state is listed.

All courts previously required the debtor to prepare a list of the creditors' names and addresses in rows and columns which corresponded to sheets of mailing labels. To properly align the rows and columns of addresses, it was necessary to take a blank sheet of paper and insert it in a typewriter with a MAILING MATRIX behind it. (see form 18, p.200.) A sheet of addresses prepared in this manner allowed the clerk to photo-copy the list onto a mailing label sheet. If your court still uses a MAILING MATRIX, you can use form 18 to prepare it; however, be sure to check with the court clerk to be sure you know how to properly prepare it.

The bankruptcy courts in many states have entered the computer age. These courts take a more simply prepared list of creditors' names and addresses, scan them into a computer, then have the computer generate the addressed envelopes. These courts typically have detailed instructions about how the list is to be prepared and submitted by the debtor. To get these instructions, check with the court clerk or the website listed above.

COURT PROCEDURES 7

It is important to familiarize yourself with the steps you need to take to file your papers with the court clerk. This chapter not only gives you these steps, but also explains the meeting your creditors will have and how the court hearing will proceed.

FILING WITH THE COURT CLERK AND NOTIFYING CREDITORS

Once all of your papers have been prepared, you are ready to file them with the court clerk. This is not difficult, however, things will go smoother if you are organized and know what you can expect.

FINDING THE CLERK'S OFFICE

By now you should have found out where the bankruptcy court is located. If not, the first place to check is the government listings in your local telephone directory. Look in the U.S. Government section for "Bankruptcy Court," "District Court," or "Clerk of the District Court." If this fails, there is probably a general U.S. government "information" listing that you can call to get the location and mailing address of the bankruptcy court clerk's office.

Only a few cities in each state have a federal court, so you may need to do some digging to find the one closest to you. If you are having trouble, try calling the law library at the county courthouse in your county, or try your local public library.

WHAT TO BRING

There are checklists in Appendix B to indicate what you should bring with you to the court clerk's office when you go to file your papers.

FILING

Although it is possible to file by mail, it is strongly advised that you go to the clerk's office and file in-person. It is easier to establish a friendly relationship in-person, and the more time you spend at the bankruptcy court the more comfortable you will feel with the entire process.

As you enter the clerk's office, look around for any signs that may help you figure out exactly where to go. There may be several windows, which may be marked for different purposes, such as "Filing," "Cashier," "File Check-out," etc. Go to the appropriate window, or to any window if you are uncertain, and tell the clerk "I'd like to file a Chapter 7," or "I'd like to file a Chapter 13."

The clerk will take your papers and examine them (or refer you to the proper window, where that clerk will take them). If everything looks in order, the clerk will then tell you how to go about paying the filing fee. Either that clerk will handle the payment, or you will be directed to the cashier's window.

You will pay the filing fee, and receive a receipt. The clerk will also assign a case number, and will stamp or write the number on your papers. The case number should also be on your receipt. Your papers are now filed.

If the clerk determines that something is not correct with your papers, you will be told what is wrong. *Do not argue with the clerk.* The clerk controls your access to the bankruptcy system, and you don't want to make an enemy of the clerk. Clerks cannot give you legal advice, but they will usually tell you what is wrong with your papers, and give you some idea of how you can fix the problem.

The kind of problem the clerk will identify is one of form, such as you forgot to sign something, forgot to fill in a space, need another type of form, need to submit an extra copy, etc. All you can do is find out what the clerk wants, then do it. You may be able to correct the problem at the clerk's office.

If you try to satisfy the clerk, but are still getting your papers rejected or do not understand what is required, you may want to consult a lawyer. You can also politely tell the clerk that you are not understanding the problem, and ask him or her to explain it again, or have another clerk try to explain it to you.

Although most clerks are pleasant, helpful people, you sometimes run into a simply nasty clerk. You must still be polite, and try to win over the clerk; but if this does not work there is nothing wrong with asking for the clerk's supervisor. Just do not get angry under any circumstances. Remain calm and polite.

STOPPING PAYMENTS

If you have not already stopped making payments, you should stop once your petition is filed (except for payments on any secured debts if you want to keep the property). From this point on, all payments for anything must be approved by the trustee. It is all right to buy food, gas for your car so you can get to work, and to pay for any necessary medical expenses, but that is about all.

It will take awhile to have a trustee appointed, but as soon as you receive a notice in the mail with the name of the trustee, contact the trustee as soon as possible. Tell the trustee that you just wanted to make an initial contact, and ask him or her if it is all right to pay any bills you feel you need to pay. Also ask the trustee any other questions you have. If you are continuing to make payments on secured property (such as your mortgage or car payment), mention this to the trustee.

AUTOMATIC STAY

Filing your petition operates as an *automatic stay*, which prohibits your creditors from taking any collection action, or from cutting off any services to you. Once your petition is filed, you may want to be sure to get your creditors off your back by sending them a letter notifying them that you have filed. Letter 2, found in Appendix E of this book, is a form letter for this purpose. (see letter 2, p.208.)

Space is left at the top for the date and the creditor's address. Sign your name at the bottom, and below your name, type in your name, address, and account number. If you have a particularly bothersome creditor, you may want to send the letter by certified, return-receipt mail. Let the trustee know if any creditors continue to bother you.

CREDITORS' MEETING

After you have filed your case, the clerk will do several things. Using the master address list you provided, and the information in your supporting documents, the clerk will send a notice to all of your creditors telling them that you have filed for bankruptcy. A trustee will also be appointed to your case, who will then schedule a meeting of creditors. Copies of any documents issued by the clerk or the trustee will be sent to you. Read them carefully, and call the clerk's office if you don't understand them. Most of these papers will not require you to do anything, but some may require some type of response.

You may also receive copies of any papers your creditors may file with the clerk. Again, these don't require you to do anything, but keep copies anyway.

You will receive a notice of the date, time and place of the meeting of creditors, which you must attend. The nature of this meeting varies slightly depending upon whether you selected a Chapter 7 or a Chapter 13 proceeding.

CHAPTER 7 CASES

In a large number of cases no creditors come to the meeting. The trustee will review your papers and ask you some questions. The questions are usually to verify what is in your papers, or to fill in information that you may have left out.

A few days before the meeting, call the trustee and ask him or her to tell you what information you should bring to the creditors meeting. In all cases, be sure to bring copies of all the papers you filed and all the papers you have received regarding your case. You should also bring tax returns and other documents that support the information in the papers you filed. Each court may have its own particular requirements, which is why it is a good idea to ask the trustee.

If creditors do attend the meeting, they also have the right to ask you questions. A creditor's usual concern is whether you have identified all of your non-exempt property, and whether such property has been turned over to the trustee for sale. Answer all of the questions honestly, as you will be under oath.

If the trustee decides that your any non-exempt property is not worth enough to justify trying to sell it, he or she may *abandon* the property. This means that you will get to keep it, even though it is not exempt.

CHAPTER 13
CASES

Creditors are more likely to attend the meeting in a Chapter 13 case than in a Chapter 7 case. They are concerned about getting the most out of your proposed payment plan. They will ask questions about the reasonableness of your payment plan, and the likelihood that you will be able to carry it out. The trustee will also ask some questions. Again, you are under oath, so answer honestly.

If the creditors and the trustee approve of your plan, it will be accepted by the court. If the plan is not approved, you may either negotiate changes in the plan to make it acceptable, stick to your plan and let the judge decide if it is acceptable, or convert your case to a Chapter 7 bankruptcy. To convert your case, see Section 8, page 82 of this book.

Once your plan is approved, the trustee will probably order that the payments be deducted directly from your paycheck by your employer. This amount will be sent to the trustee, who will make the required payments to the individual creditors.

Until the paycheck deduction goes into effect, however, you are responsible for making certain that the payments are made. Unless the court orders something different, payments must begin 30 days after you file your plan with the court. This may be before the creditors meeting, in which case you should still begin your payments. If your plan ends up not being approved, the creditors will be required to refund any payments you have made.

COURT HEARING AND DISCHARGE

Depending upon the procedures in your particular bankruptcy court, you may or may not have to appear before the judge. If the trustee determines that everything is in order, you may receive a discharge without having to attend a hearing.

CHAPTER 7 CASES
In a Chapter 7 bankruptcy, once you have done all that is required to settle the case (turned over your non-exempt assets to the trustee, paid the filing fee and any other costs required, etc.) an order will be entered discharging all of your dischargeable debts. As has already been discussed, you will not be discharged from the following types of debts:

- taxes, fines, or penalties owed to the government;

- alimony or child support;

- certain types of student loans;

- obligations as a result of criminal or fraudulent actions; or,

- any debts that were not declared in your bankruptcy, or which involve creditors not timely notified.

CHAPTER 13 CASES
In a Chapter 13 case, you will be entitled to a discharge once you have completed all of the payments required by your payment plan. This is more likely to require a brief court hearing with the judge.

ALL CASES
In either case, the judge will probably only:

- talk to you about the effects of the bankruptcy discharge;

- caution you to avoid getting in debt again;

- possibly ask a few questions to assure himself that everything has been done properly; and,

- make sure that you understand the meaning of the discharge.

Your particular bankruptcy court may even have mass discharge hearings, in which many debtors are discharged at the same time and no questions are asked. All the judge does is give everyone a brief lecture about how your debts are now discharged, and how you should avoid getting into financial trouble again.

SPECIAL CIRCUMSTANCES 8

This section will discuss several matters that do not apply to most simple bankruptcy cases. If any of these situations apply to your case, you may want to discuss them with a lawyer. Of course you should take a look at how much you may save, in contrast to how much a lawyer may cost you. The first two items mentioned have forms in Appendix D of this book, and you can probably do them without an attorney. However, the other items will often require an attorney's assistance.

AMENDING YOUR PAPERWORK

If, after you file your VOLUNTARY PETITION (form 1) and other papers, you discover that you have made an error, you may amend whatever papers are necessary to correct the error. This will involve completing the AMENDMENT COVER SHEET, as well as whatever forms you need to amend. (see form 21, p.203.)

Some courts will require you to fully complete the new form, while others will allow you to simply note the item being changed. You will need to call the court clerk to find out which you need to do. At the same time, ask the clerk if there is any filing fee for the amended form.

To complete the AMENDMENT COVER SHEET (form 21):

- After the first sentence, type in the name of the form or forms you are amending. Be sure to also complete the top portion of the form, as well as the date and signature portions at the bottom.

- Attach the amended forms containing the new or changed information.

- You need to be sure to check whether the new information on one form also requires new information on other forms, and to include all forms that need changing. Also, certain changes may mean that you need to re-notify creditors, especially if the creditors' meeting has already been held.

  Check with the trustee or clerk to see if you need to re-notify all of your creditors. If you do, you will need to send a copy of your AMENDMENT COVER SHEET and the changed documents to each creditor, and will need to complete a PROOF OF SERVICE BY MAIL (CERTIFICATE OF MAILING). (see form 20, p.202.)

To complete form 20:

- ☞ Fill in the title of the documents you send.

- ☞ Fill in the name and address of all the creditors or others you send copies to.

If the creditors' meeting has already been held, another meeting may need to be scheduled.

CHANGING FROM CHAPTER 13 TO CHAPTER 7

If you filed your case under Chapter 13 of the bankruptcy act, and have determined that you need to convert your case to Chapter 7, you need to complete a MOTION TO CONVERT TO CHAPTER 7. (see form 22, p.204.) This form only requires you to complete the top portion and the date and signature portion. At the time you file this form, also include any other forms needed for a Chapter 7 bankruptcy as described in Section 6, pages 49-73 of this book [usually only the CHAPTER 7 INDIVIDUAL DEBTOR'S STATEMENT OF INTENTION. (see form 16, p.198.)]

Lien Avoidance

Lien avoidance is a procedure that allows a debtor to keep certain property that might otherwise be subject to repossession. Before reading about this any further, you should know that this is not available if you live in the following states: Kentucky, Louisiana, Maryland, Mississippi, Tennessee, and Utah. Also, it is only available in Connecticut, Texas, and Washington if you use the Federal Bankruptcy Exemptions. With the possible exception of Connecticut, it is most likely that you will find the state exemptions more of an advantage in these states, especially if you own a home. Furthermore, lien avoidance only applies to exempt property, and you can't avoid more than the exemption allows.

Next, you need to see if you have either of the two types of liens to which this can apply:

1. those created by a court judgment; and

2. those created when you used property you already had as security for a new loan.

You may not avoid a lien if you took out the loan in order to buy the secured piece of property. Therefore, if you have no court judgments, and your secured debts all relate to the items you purchased, you are not eligible for lien avoidance.

There are three other important limitations on the use of lien avoidance.

1. You cannot avoid a lien on your vehicle, unless it is used as a part of your business (which does not include use to get to and from work).

2. If the lien is for more than the exemption amount for that item, the lien will only be reduced and the creditor may still repossess if the amount remaining isn't paid immediately.

3. Lien avoidance can only be accomplished by filing more papers with the court, possibly leading to a court battle with the creditor, and even the necessity for an appraisal of the property.

Redemption

Redemption is where you agree to pay the creditor a lump sum, based upon the market value of a piece of exempt property. This is generally only advisable if the property is worth less than the amount owed on the loan. Instead of paying off the full loan, you only pay the amount the property is worth. This is done because if the creditor repossesses the property, he will only be able to sell it for the market value as the remainder of the loan is discharged in the bankruptcy.

However, there are limitations here also. Three conditions must be met:

1. the debt must be a consumer debt, meaning it is for personal use, as opposed to business use;

2. it must be for tangible, personal property (as opposed to items like stocks and bonds); and,

3. you must be claiming the property as exempt, or the trustee must abandon the property (which is usually done because the property is of little value).

Reaffirming a Debt

Reaffirming a debt (also called *reaffirmation*) is where you and your creditor agree that the debt will still be owed after the bankruptcy and that you will continue to make payments. This requires a written agreement, signed by you and your creditor, and must contain certain provisions. A preferable alternative to this is for you to bring your payments current before filing for bankruptcy, and keep up your payments so the loan is not in default.

Reaffirmation should be a last resort, as it takes negotiating with the creditor, leaves you still liable for a debt, and requires the preparation of a written legal agreement. Economically, reaffirmation often only makes sense if the loan is not current, you owe considerably less money than the property is worth, and the property is exempt.

LAWSUITS

If you are involved in a lawsuit in which anyone is suing for money (such as a lawsuit for personal injuries or to collect a debt), to foreclose or repossess your property, or to evict you from your residence, you need to immediately notify the court and the creditor that you have filed for bankruptcy. This will bring the lawsuit to a dead stop, and your creditor will have to get the bankruptcy court judge's permission to continue with the lawsuit.

The formal way to do this is to file a form called a SUGGESTION OF BANKRUPTCY, with the court where the lawsuit is pending. (see form 19, p.201.) *Do not* file this form in the bankruptcy court. You will need to complete the top portion of the form in exactly the same manner as your other court papers in the lawsuit read (*not* the way the bankruptcy papers read), and file it with the clerk of that court (*not* the bankruptcy clerk).

PENSIONS AND RETIREMENT PLANS

The question here is whether you can keep your pension plan as exempt property. As you are about to see, this can get very complicated, so you would be wise to consult a bankruptcy attorney, especially if you have a sizable pension plan that you are relying upon to see you through retirement.

You need to determine if your pension plan is an *ERISA-qualified* plan. You can find this out by asking your employer's pension plan administrator. Such plans are covered by the Employee Retirement Income Security Act (or *ERISA* for short).

The United States Supreme Court has caused a great deal of confusion over whether an ERISA-qualified plan is exempt, although it now appears to have straightened things out.

This confusion began in 1990, when the Supreme Court said that states cannot exempt ERISA-qualified pension plans, because only the U.S. government can pass laws concerning such plans. It then became a complicated matter to decide if you could exempt your ERISA-qualified benefits. This involved determining whether your state would allow you to use the Federal Non-Bankruptcy Exemptions, whether certain other complicated conditions existed, and whether you should do this considering your other exempt property.

If you did not live in one of the states allowing the Federal Non-Bankruptcy Exemptions, bankruptcy courts in certain other states had decided that ERISA-qualified benefits were not a part of the bankruptcy estate. At that point it seemed that the only safe bet was to consult an attorney to find out what you had to do in your state.

Fortunately, in June of 1992, the United States Supreme Court issued a new ruling that ERISA-qualified pension plans are exempt from creditors by the ERISA law itself. Therefore, if you have an ERISA-qualified plan, claim it as exempt on SCHEDULE C - PROPERTY CLAIMED AS EXEMPT. (see form 6, p.174.) In the second column, headed SPECIFY LAW PROVIDING EACH EXEMPTION, type in: "11 U.S.C. §541(c)(2); 29 U.S.C. §1056(d)(1); and *Patterson v. Shumate*, 112 S.Ct. 2242 (1992)." These are the references to the federal law and the Supreme Court opinion making ERISA-qualified plans exempt.

If your state also has a law exempting ERISA-qualified plans (see your state's listing in Appendix A), type in the reference to that law also.

If you do not have an ERISA-qualified plan, you need to see if your state exemptions cover your plan. If your plan is not covered by a state exemption, you may want to find out if you can cash in your pension. You can then use the money to buy exempt property (but be sure to read Section 4, page 40 of this book before you try this).

PENSIONS AND DIVORCE

If you were divorced, your pension plan benefits may have been divided between you and your ex-spouse. If your plan is not exempt, whether your ex-spouse still gets his or her share may depend upon how the plan was divided in the divorce case. If the plan was divided by a *Qualified Domestic Relations Order* (or QDRO, which is pronounced "quadro" by lawyers), your ex-spouse will still receive his or her share. However, if the court simply ordered you to pay your ex-spouse his or her share, you may be able to discharge this debt to your ex-spouse in bankruptcy. If you want to do this, you need to consult a bankruptcy lawyer.

AFTER YOUR DISCHARGE 9

Once you receive your discharge, you need to think about the future. The two main things you need to do are make sure that you do not get into financial trouble again, and start building credit again.

HANDLING YOUR FINANCES

From the INCOME AND EXPENSE WORKSHEET (worksheet 1) you have an idea of how to prepare a budget. Use the MONTHLY BUDGET in Appendix C to help keep your financial matters under control. (see worksheet 4, p.162.) Make additional copies of worksheet 4 to use in the months ahead. Your budgeting has three main goals:

1. assuring that you aren't spending more than you earn;

2. assuring that you will have the money available when the bill is due; or

3. developing a savings plan.

You should have a checking account. If you do not, shop around for a bank with the lowest minimum balance for free checking, or the lowest checking charges. If you are eligible to join a credit union, you will probably find they have the best deal around.

There are dozens of different checking account arrangements, so compare.

Use the top line of the first column of the MONTHLY BUDGET to write in the total amount in your checking account. (see worksheet 4, p.162.) Your job is to decide which of the debts listed needs to be paid before your next paycheck, and how much of the total needs to be assigned to each of those debts.

Use the other columns to allocate your next several paychecks to your debts. Hopefully, after deducting all of the debt payments from the amounts in the top column, something will be left over.

Ideally, experts say, you should save approximately 10% of each paycheck. For many people this seems impossible. But that is no excuse for not trying to save something. If you have never saved, try it for awhile. You may be surprised to find out that the feeling you get from looking at a bank account balance with an emergency cushion of $200 or $1,000 is as good as the feeling you'd get from spending that money.

The important thing is not to buy something unless you know exactly where you will get the money to pay for it when the bill is due. Whenever you think about buying on credit, look at your budget and ask yourself where the money will come from. It certainly cannot come from the rent money, or from the food money. It should only come from the "Spending" money, such as from next week's paycheck. If so, then subtract that amount from the "Spending" line in the column for next week's check, and write it on one of the lines for "Credit Payments," also writing in the name of the store or other credit card involved.

OBTAINING CREDIT

One of the problems, or maybe it's a blessing in disguise, of going through a bankruptcy is that it will be difficult to obtain credit. During the bankruptcy you found out what life is like without the use of credit, and it is a good idea to do without credit until you are sure that you can keep your finances under control. However, in our society, credit is almost essential if one is to improve one's standard of living.

Buying a home is frequently a better deal than renting one. Also, some essential items, such as cars, are very difficult to pay for in cash. So it is a good idea to begin establishing some credit once you have things (including your spending habits) under control.

LOCAL STORE
CREDIT CARDS

One way to begin is to apply for a credit card from a local store. Almost every type of store now has its own credit cards, particularly local department stores and hardware stores. Many of these stores will issue a temporary card immediately upon filling out an application. Go into the store, fill out the application (which usually only asks your name, address, and where you work), then buy something immediately with the temporary card. Even if the application is later rejected, you still have an obligation to make the payments on the item you bought, and that repayment will be something positive in your new credit record. You can always do the same thing the next time you need to buy something at that store. Eventually, your timely payment will be noticed and you will get an application for a permanent card approved.

MAJOR CREDIT
CARDS

Until you get a few local cards, and establish a payment record on each, you should avoid applying for a major card (such as VISA or Mastercard), and avoid applying for a card at a major, nationwide department store (such as Sears or J.C Penney). Such applications will almost certainly be rejected.

BORROWING
FROM YOUR
BANK

Another way to establish credit is to borrow against your own money. If you can accumulate some money in a savings account, the bank will probably allow you to borrow money against the savings account. Once you pay back the money, you've taken the first step toward establishing a positive credit history. You will have to pay a little interest, but the object here is to establish credit, not make a brilliant deal.

Example: Say you have $500 in a savings account. Borrow $250 against the account for a period of 30 days. Take the $250 and put it in your checking account. At the end of the 30 days, write a check to pay off the loan (even at an annual interest rate of 22%, this will mean writing a check for about $254.59). You will be paying $4.59 interest for the privilege of establishing some credit, which is not very expensive.

You are now ready to wisely deal with your financial situation and build a healthy credit history with your new credit. The MONTHLY BUDGET will help keep you on track with your spending and your future financial health.

Glossary

A

automatic stay. A provision in the federal bankruptcy law that makes it illegal for creditors to make any attempt to collect a debt once a person files for bankruptcy. Creditors must then ask the bankruptcy court's permission to resume collection efforts.

B

blue book. A common term for books that list the market value of various types of property, such as cars and boats.

C

Chapter 7 bankruptcy. A chapter of the bankruptcy code providing for the discharge of debts.

Chapter 13 bankruptcy. A chapter of the bankruptcy code allowing a debtor to create a plan to repay some or all of his or her debts.

codebtor. A person who is jointly obligated with another to repay a debt.

community property. A type of property ownership created by statute in some states, in which property is owned in common by a husband and wife as a kind of marital partnership.

contingent debt. A debt that will only be owed upon the occurrence of some future event.

cosigned debt. A debt that a second party agrees to pay if the first party fails to pay.

creditor. One who is owed a debt.

D

discharge. (1.) The elimination of an obligation to repay a debt. (2.) The release of a debtor from further oversight by the bankruptcy court at the end of a bankruptcy case.

dischargeable debts. Debts that may be discharged in a bankruptcy proceeding.

disputed debt. A debt that the debtor does not believe is owed, or in which there is a disagreement over the amount owed.

E

executory contract. A contract in which the obligations of either or both parties have not been completed.

exempt property. Property that may not be taken and sold to satisfy a debt.

F

foreclosure. The legal process of taking real estate in order to satisfy a debt secured by a mortgage.

future interest. An interest in real property, whereby possession will occur in the future (such as after a life estate is completed).

H

homestead. A person's primary home and place of residence, which, in most states, is wholly or partially exempt from the claims of creditors (unless the creditor holds a mortgage on the property).

L

lien avoidance. A procedure, in certain cases and in certain states, whereby a debtor is allowed to keep property that would otherwise be subject to repossession.

life estate. An interest in land, whereby the person holding the life estate is allowed the use of the land during his or her life. Upon that person's death, the land goes to someone designated by the original owner.

N

non-dischargeable debts. Debts that may not be discharged in a bankruptcy proceeding.

non-exempt property. Property that is not exempt from the claims of creditors.

nonpriority claim. The claim of any creditor who is not the type of creditor given priority for payment by the bankruptcy code.

P

priority claim. The claim of a creditor who is given priority for payment by the bankruptcy code. Priority claims are paid before nonpriority claims.

R

reaffirmation. When a debtor agrees that a debt will still be owed after bankruptcy, even though the debt could have been discharged.

redemption. When a debtor and creditor agree that the debtor will pay a certain sum and will be allowed to keep an item of property that secured the debt. In essence, the debtor is buying back the property.

repossession. The legal process of taking personal property (such as a car or household furniture) in order to satisfy a debt secured by the particular item of personal property.

S

secured debt. A debt that is guaranteed by a particular piece of real or personal property, whereby the creditor may take the property if the debt is not repaid.

set-off. An amount owed by a creditor to a debtor, which is applied to reduce the amount of the debt owed.

T

tools of trade. The legal term for items of property used in a person's business, trade, or profession.

trustee. The person appointed by the court to oversee a bankruptcy case.

U

unliquidated debt. A debt that is recognized by both debtor and creditor, but the exact amount owed is yet to be determined.

unsecured debt. A debt that is not guaranteed by any particular piece of real or personal property.

W

wage-earner plan. A common name for a Chapter 13 bankruptcy.

APPENDIX A
EXEMPTIONS (FEDERAL AND STATE-BY-STATE)

This appendix is used to find what exemptions are available to you. In addition to listing the exemptions available in each state, the federal exemptions are also listed. There are two types of federal exemptions, one is called *Federal Bankruptcy Exemptions* and the other is called *Federal Non-Bankruptcy Exemptions*.

The Federal Bankruptcy Exemptions are not available in all states, so check the list at the beginning of the Federal Bankruptcy Exemption listing. If the Federal Bankruptcy Exemptions are allowed in your state, you will need to choose between the state exemptions and the Federal Bankruptcy Exemptions. You will need to compare the state exemptions to the Federal Bankruptcy Exemptions to determine which way will allow you to keep more property. In most cases the state exemptions will be better for you, but make the comparison just to be sure.

The Federal Non-Bankruptcy Exemptions are available along with your state's exemptions.

Under the listing for each state you will find a notation as to whether the Federal Bankruptcy Exemptions may be used. Under the heading MISCELLANEOUS, there is also a reminder for you to use any of the Federal Non-Bankruptcy Exemptions that may apply to you.

The following listings give the section number for the applicable state law, and the exemption that relates to that section. At the beginning of each state's section, you will find information (with an example in parentheses) about how to write the statute reference in the second column of Schedule C.

If no amount is stated, the amount of that type of property you may claim is unlimited. Where an amount is stated, you may only claim up to that amount as exempt. If you want to be sure you understand the exemption, go to your library and look up the actual language in that section of your state's law.

Many states' law books have volume numbers on them. Where applicable, advice is given to ignore the volume number because it is not part of the official manner of referring to the law in your state.

Doubling Exemptions. Some states allow a husband and wife to each claim a separate exemption.

Example: If an automobile is exempt up to $3,000 in equity, the husband and wife may each claim an auto up to $3,000. This is referred to as *doubling* the exemption.

An asterisk (*) after an item indicates that doubling is specifically *prohibited* by law. Two asterisks (**) indicates that doubling is specifically *approved* by law. No notation indicates that the law does not state whether doubling is permitted, so you may want to list the exemption for both husband and wife, and see if the trustee accepts it.

"ERISA" Pension Benefits. These are benefits from retirement plans that qualify under the federal Employee Retirement Income Security Act ("ERISA" for short). Your employer or retirement plan administrator can tell you whether your plan is an ERISA-qualified plan.

Most states have laws providing for a bankruptcy exemption for ERISA-qualified retirement plan benefits. Whether the states can exempt such plans has been the source of much dispute in past years. The Supreme Court has said that ERISA-qualified pension plans may be exempted by the states.

You should check with a bankruptcy lawyer if you run into any problems with the trustee or judge regarding such a plan. Your retirement plan can be a vital asset and you should take all necessary steps to preserve it and protect it from your creditors.

Warning: The exemption charts in this appendix are not guaranteed to be current, nor are they guaranteed to contain every possible exemption. These charts are designed to include the basic exemptions to cover the most usual situations. Legislatures may change the exemptions at any time, and there may be obscure exemptions applicable to very narrow situations. Your local public library, or law library (usually found at your county courthouse) should have a current copy of your state's laws. Your law library should also have books about bankruptcy which should contain the most recent exemptions. If you think you have a particular asset which may be entitled to an exemption not listed, or feel you need an exemption explained in more detail, you should consult an attorney.

WEBSITES

You may find all states' statutes on the Internet, although they can vary dramatically in user-friendliness. Some of these sites are maintained by the state government, and others are maintained by private companies or law firms. For a some states, the laws are also available by paying for a subscription service. A single site, **http://www.findlaw.com**, provides access to all of the state websites. The sites listed below for individual states are the same sites that Findlaw will take you to, but they are provided here because you may wish to skip a few of the steps in getting to them through Findlaw. These sites may change at any time, so if you have any problems accessing a site listed below, try the Findlaw site. Additional help in navigating a particular state's website may also be included below.

All States	http://www.findlaw.com Once you get to the Findlaw site, click on "US State Resources," then click on the name of the state you want, then click on "Primary Materials-Cases, Codes and Regulations," then click on the state code or statutes.
Alabama	http://www.legislature.state.al.us/CodeofAlabama/1975/coatoc.htm
Alaska	http://old-www.legis.state.ak.us/cgi-bin/folioisa.dll/stattx00?
Arizona	http://www.azleg.state.az.us/ars/ars.htm#Listing
Arkansas	http://www.arkleg.state.ar.us/newsdcode/lpext.dll?f=templates&fn=main-h.htm&20 Click on folder named "arcode."
California	You can try to get information through the Findlaw site, but there doesn't seem to be a simple way to access the Codes by section numbers.
Colorado	http://64.78.178.125/stat01/index.htm
Connecticut	http://www.cslib.org/psaindex.htm Click on "Browse the Table Of Contents," then scroll down and click on the title you want (for example "Title 52"), then scroll down and click on the chapter (for example "906 Postjudgment Proceedings"). You may need to use trial and error on the chapter number to find the section number you want. Chapter numbers are of no significance when using the statute books, but they are used for the online statutes.
Delaware	http://198.187.12/delaware/lpext.dll?f-templates&fn=tools-contents.htm&cp=Infobase&2.0
District of Columbia	http://dccode.westgroup.com/home/dccodes/default.wl
Florida	http://www.leg.state.fl.us/statutes/index.cfm?Mode=ViewStatutes&Submenu=1
Georgia	http://www.ganet.org/services/ocode/ocgsearch.htm
Hawaii	http://www.capitol.hawaii.gov/hrscurrent/?press1=docs
Idaho	http://www3.state.id.us/idstat/TOC/idstTOC.html
Illinois	http://www.legis.state.il.us/ilcs/chapterlist.html.
Indiana	http://www.ai.org/legislative/ic/code/
Iowa	http://www2.legis.state.ia.us/IACODE/2001/
Kansas	http://www.accesskansas.org/legislative/statutes/index.cgi
Kentucky	http://162.114.4.13/krs/title.htm
Louisiana	http://www.legis.state.la.us/tsrs/search.htm
Maine	http://janus.state.me.us/legis/statutes
Maryland	http://mlis.state.md.us/cgi-win/web_statutes.exe
Massachusetts	http://www.state.ma.us/legis/laws/mgl/index.htm
Michigan	http://MichiganLegislature.org/law/Default.asp
Minnesota	http://www.leg.state.mn.us/leg/statutes.htm
Mississippi	http://www.sos.state.ms.us/policy_admin/mscode/index.html
Missouri	http://www.moga.state.mo.us/homestat.htm

Montana	http://statedocs.msl.state.mt.us/cgi-bin/om_isapi.dll?client ID=5341&infobase=mca_99.nfo&softpage=Browse_Frame_Pg
Nebraska	http://statutes.unicam.state.ne.us/Statutes/lpext.dll?f=templates&fn=main-h.htm&vid=10.104852FEnu&2.0
Nevada	http://www.leg.state.nv.us/NRS/index.cfm
New Hampshire	http://sudoc.nhsl.lib.nh.us/rsa/#index
New Jersey	http://www.njleg.state.nj.us/cgi-bin/om_isapi.dll?client ID=395992&depth=2&expandheadings=off&headingswithhits=on&infobase=statutes.nfo&softpage=TOC_Frame_Pg42
	This website is very difficult to use, especially if you are trying to bring up a particular section number.
New Mexico	http://198.187.128.12/newmexico/lpext.dll/Infobase2/10a2?fn=document-frame.htm&f-templates&2.0
New York	Findlaw site: http://caselaw.lp.findlaw.com/nycodes/index.html
	NY State Assembly site: http://assembly.state.ny.us/leg/?cl=0
	For either site, click on the subject you want, then try to figure out which "article" or "part" number you need. As most statutes have "section" numbers, this can be difficult to figure out.
North Carolina	http://www.ncga.state.nc.us/Statutes/toc-1.html
North Dakota	http://www.state.nd.us/lr/statutes/centurycode.html
Ohio	http://onlinedocs.andersonpublishing.com/revisedcode/
Oklahoma	Attorney General: http://oklegal.onenet.net/statutes.basic.html
	Oklahoma State Courts Network:
	http://www.oscn.net/applications/oscn/index.asp?ftdb=STOKST&level=1
Oregon	http://www.leg.state.or.us/ors/orstoc.html
Pennsylvania	http://members.aol.com/StatutesPA/Index.html
Rhode Island:	http:www.rilin.state.ri.us/Statutes/Statutes.html
South Carolina	http://www.lpitr.state.sc.us/code/statmast.htm
South Dakota	http://legis.state.sd.us/statutes/index.cfm
Tennessee	http://198.187.128.12/tennessee/lpext.dll?f=templates&fn=main-h.htm&2.0
Texas	http://www.capitol.state.tx.us/statutes/statutes.html
Utah	http://www.le.state.ut.us/~code/code.htm
Vermont	Statutes, court rules, etc.: http://www.leg.state.vt.us/statutes/titles.htm
	Statutes only: http://198.187.128.12/vermont/lpext.dll?f=temmplates&fn=main-h.htm&2.0
Virginia	http://leg1.state.va.us/cgi-bin/legp504.exe?000+cod+TOC
Washington	http://www.leg.wa.gov/wsladm/rcw.cfm#RCW_by_Title
West Virginia	http://www.legis.state.wv.us/Code/toc.html
	This is a terrible website; you can't search by section number, but only by words and phrases.
Wisconsin	http://www.legis.state.wi.us/rsb/Statutes.html
Wyoming	http://legisweb.state.wy.us/statutes/statutes.htm

FEDERAL BANKRUPTCY EXEMPTIONS

The following Federal Bankruptcy Exemptions are available (as an alternative to the state exemptions) if you live in one of the following states:

Arkansas	Massachusetts	New Mexico	Texas
Connecticut	Michigan	Pennsylvania	Vermont
District of Columbia	Minnesota	Rhode Island	Washington
Hawaii	New Jersey	South Carolina	Wisconsin

If you use these exemptions, however, you cannot use the exemptions listed under your state. Be sure to compare these exemptions to those in the listing for your state, and use whichever allows you to keep more of your property. Remember, the Federal Bankruptcy Exemptions can be doubled by husband and wife.

The following section numbers relate to Title 11 of the United States Code, which is abbreviated "11 U.S.C." followed by the appropriate section ("§" is the symbol for *section* number, and "§§" is the symbol for *sections* (more than one).) An example is: "11 U.S.C. § 522(d)(1)." Only the section number is used below on the left side listing.

HOMESTEAD (**)
522(d)(1)   Real property, including mobile homes and coops, up to $15,000. Unused portion, up to $7,500, may be used for other property.

PERSONAL PROPERTY (**)
522(d)(2)   Motor vehicle up to $2,400.
522(d)(3)   Animals, crops, clothing, appliances and furnishings, books, household goods, and musical instruments up to $400 per item, and up to $8,000 total.
522(d)(4)   Jewelry up to $1,000.
522(d)(5) $800 of any property, and unused portion of homestead up to $7,500.
522(d)(9)   Health aids.
522(d)(11)(B)   Wrongful death recovery for person you depended upon.
522(d)(11)(D)   Personal injury recovery up to 15,000, except for pain and suffering or for pecuniary loss.
522(d)(11)(E)   Lost earning payments.

PENSIONS
522(d)(10)(E)   ERISA-qualified benefits needed for support.

PUBLIC BENEFITS
522(d)(10)(A)   Public assistance, Social Security, Veteran's benefits, Unemployment Compensation.
522(d)(11)(A)   Crime victim's compensation.

TOOLS OF TRADE (**)
522(d)(6)   Implements, books and tools of trade, up to $1,500.

ALIMONY AND CHILD SUPPORT
522(d)(10)(D)   Alimony and child support needed for support.

INSURANCE
522(d)(7)   Unmatured life insurance policy.
522(d)(8)   Life insurance policy with loan value up to $8,000 (**).
522(d)(10)(C)   Disability, unemployment or illness benefits.
522(d)(11)(C)   Life insurance payments for a person you depended on, which you need for support.

FEDERAL NON-BANKRUPTCY EXEMPTIONS

You may only use these exemptions if you choose the exemptions listed under your state. You may not use these if you choose to use the Federal Bankruptcy Exemptions listed on the previous page.

RETIREMENT BENEFITS

50 U.S.C. §403	CIA employees.
5 U.S.C. §8346	Civil Service employees.
22 U.S.C. §4060	Foreign service employees.
10 U.S.C. §1440	Military service employees.
45 U.S.C.§.231m	Railroad workers.
42 U.S.C. §407	Social Security benefits.
38 U.S.C. §3101	Veteran's benefits.

SURVIVOR'S BENEFITS

10 U.S.C. §1450	Military service.
28 U.S.C. §376	Judges, U.S. court directors.
33 U.S.C. §775	Lighthouse workers.

DEATH AND DISABILITY BENEFITS

5 U.S.C. §8130	U.S. Government employees.
33 U.S.C. §916	Longshoremen, harbor workers.
42 U.S.C. §1717	Military service.

MISCELLANEOUS

10 U.S.C. §1035	Military deposits to savings accounts (while on permanent duty outside the U.S.).
15 U.S.C. §1673	75% of earned but unpaid wages (Judge may approve more).
25 U.S.C. §543 & 545	Klamath Indians tribe benefits.
38 U.S.C. §770(g)	Military group life insurance.
45 U.S.C. §352(e)	Railroad workers' unemployment.
46 U.S.C. §11110	Seamen's clothing.
46 U.S.C. §11111	Seamen's wages (while on a voyage and pursuant to a written contract).

ALABAMA

Code of Alabama, Title 6, Chapter 10 (C.A. §6-10-2). Ignore volume numbers; look for "title" numbers.

HOMESTEAD

6-10-2   Real property or mobile home, up to $5,000. Property can't exceed 160 acres.(**) Must record homestead declaration. 6-10-20.

PERSONAL PROPERTY

6-10-5   A burial place and a church pew or seat.

6-10-6   Clothing, books and family portraits and pictures, and $3,000 of any other personal property (except life insurance).

WAGES

6-10-7   75% of earned but unpaid wages. Judge may approve more for low-income debtors.

PENSIONS

12-18-10	Judges.	36-21-77	Law enforcement officers.
16-25-23	Teachers.	36-27-28	State employees.

PUBLIC BENEFITS

15-23-15	Crime victims' compensation.
25-4-140	Unemployment compensation.
25-5-86	Workers' compensation.
25-5-179	Coal miners' pneumoconiosis benefits.
31-7-2	Southeast Asian War POW's benefits.
38-4-8	AFDC and aid to blind, aged, and disabled.

TOOLS OF TRADE

31-2-78   Arms, uniforms and equipment required to be kept by state military personnel.

INSURANCE

6-10-8;

27-14-29	Life insurance proceeds if beneficiary is spouse or child of the insured.
27-14-31	Disability proceeds up to an average of $250 per month.
27-14-32	Annuities up to $250 per month.
27-15-26	Life insurance, if policy prohibits use to pay creditors.
27-30-25	Mutual aid association benefits.
27-34-27	Fraternal benefit society benefits.

MISCELLANEOUS

10-8-72	Business partnership property.
Other	Add any applicable Federal Non-Bankruptcy Exemptions.

NOTE: *The symbol "§" or "§§" stands for* section *or* sections *of the statutes or code in your state. It refers to the particular part of the statutes of code listed here to the left of all references. A law librarian can help you.*

ALASKA

Alaska Statutes, Title 9, Section 9.38.010 (A.S. §9.38.010). Ignore volume numbers; look for "title" numbers. In *In re McNutt*, 87 B.R. 84 (9th Cir. 1988), the Federal Bankruptcy Exemptions were allowed.

HOMESTEAD
9.38-010 (*) Up to $54,000.

PERSONAL PROPERTY
9.38.015 Burial plot; needed health aids; and tuition credits under advance college payment contract.
9.38.020 Motor vehicle up to $3,000, if market value is no more than $20,000; pets up to $1,000; jewelry up to $1,000; and household goods, clothing, books, musical instruments, and family portraits and heirlooms up to $3,000.
9.38.030 Personal injury and wrongful death recoveries, to the extent wages are exempt.
9.38.060 Proceeds from damaged exempt property.
34.35.105 Building materials.

WAGES
9.38.030;
9.38.050 Weekly net earnings up to $350, or up to $550 if sole wage earner in a household. If no regular pay, up to $1,400 paid in any month, or $2,200 if sole wage earner in household.

PENSIONS
9.38.015 Teachers, judicial & public employees, and elected officers, as to benefits accruing.
9.38.017 ERISA-qualified benefits, if deposited more than 120 days before filing.
9.38.030 Payments being received from other pensions.

PUBLIC BENEFITS
9.38.015 Alaska longevity bonus, crime victims' compensation and federally exempt public benefits.
23.20.405 Unemployment compensation.
23.30.160 Workers' compensation.
43.23.065 45% of Permanent Fund dividends (this is income distributed to residents from the state's natural resources).
47.25.210 General relief assistance.
47.25.395 AFDC.
47.25.550 Assistance to blind, elderly and disabled adults.

TOOLS OF TRADE
9.38.020 Implements, books or tools up to $2,800.

ALIMONY AND CHILD SUPPORT
9.38.015 Child support if received from a collection agency.
9.38.030 Alimony, to extent wages are exempt.

INSURANCE
9.38.015;
9.38.030 Medical and disability benefits.
9.38.025 Life insurance or annuity contracts up to a $10,000 loan value.
9.38.030 Life insurance proceeds to a spouse or dependent, and personal injury insurance proceeds, to extent wages are exempt.
21.84.240 Fraternal benefit society benefits.

MISCELLANEOUS
9.38.015 Liquor licenses; Alaska Fisheries limited entry permits.
9.38.100 Business partnership property.
Other Add any applicable Federal Non-Bankruptcy Exemptions.
NOTE: *The symbol "§" or "§§" stands for section or sections of the statutes or code in your state. It refers to the particular part of the statutes of code listed here to the left of all references. A law librarian can help you.*

ARIZONA

Arizona Revised Statutes Annotated, Section 33-1101 (A.R.S. §33-1101). Ignore volume numbers; look for "section" numbers.

HOMESTEAD (*)
33-1101	Up to $100,000. Includes sale proceeds up to 18 months after sale, or new home purchased, whichever occurs first. Must record homestead declaration. 33-1102.

PERSONAL PROPERTY (**)
33-1123	The following items up to $4,000 total: Two beds; one bed table, dresser and lamp for each bed; bedding; kitchen table and 4 chairs; dining table and 4 chairs; living room chair for each family member; couch; 3 living room tables and lamps; living room carpet or rug; refrigerator; stove; washer and dryer; one TV, radio or stereo (not one of each); radio alarm clock; vacuum cleaner; family portraits; and any pictures, oil paintings, and drawings created by the debtor. Additional bed, and dining chair, for each additional dependent if more than 4 persons in household.
33-1124	Food and fuel for 6 months.
33-1125	Motor vehicle up to $1,500 (or $4,000 if disabled); clothing to $500; pets, horses, milk cows and poultry to $500; books to $250; wedding and engagement rings to $1,000; musical instruments to $250; watch to $100; wheelchair and prostheses; and up to $500 total for bicycle, sewing machine, typewriter, burial plot, firearm and bible (only one of each may be kept).
33-1126	Proceeds for sold or damaged exempt property; prepaid rent or security deposit to lesser of $1,000 or 1.5 times rent (only if not claiming homestead); bank deposit to $150 in one account.

WAGES
33-1126	Earnings of minor child, unless debt is for child.
33-1131	Minimum of 75% of unpaid net wages or pension payments. Judge may allow more.

PENSIONS
9-931	Police officers.
9-968	Firefighters.
15-1628	Members of board of regents.
33-1126	ERISA-qualified benefits, if deposited more than 120 days before filing [IRA's included, *In re Herrscher*, 121 B.R. 29 (D. Ariz. 1990)].
38-762	State employees.
38-811	Elected officials.
38-850	Public safety personnel.
41-955	Rangers.

PUBLIC BENEFITS
23-783	Unemployment compensation.
23-1068	Workers' compensation.
46-208	Welfare benefits.

TOOLS OF TRADE
33-1127	Teaching aids of a teacher.
33-1130 (**)	Tools, equipment and books up to $2,500; Farm machinery, utensils, instruments of husbandry, feed, seed, grain and animals up to a total value of $2,500; and arms, uniforms and equipment you are required by law to keep.

INSURANCE
20-881	Fraternal benefit society benefits.
20-1131	Life insurance cash value up to $2,000 per dependent/$10,000 total.
20-1132	Group life insurance policy or proceeds.
33-1126 (**)	Life insurance proceeds if beneficiary is spouse or child, up to $20,000; life insurance cash value to $1,000 per dependent/$25,000 total; and health, accident or disability benefits.

MISCELLANEOUS
29-225	Business partnership property.
Other	Add any applicable Federal Non-Bankruptcy Exemptions.

ARKANSAS

Arkansas Code of 1987 Annotated, Title 16, Chapter 66, Section 16-66-210 (A.C.A. §16-66-210). Ignore volume numbers; look for "title" and "chapter" numbers. Compare Federal Bankruptcy Exemptions.

HOMESTEAD (Choose one of the following)

16-66-210 (*)	Head of family may claim: Real or personal property used as a residence; of up to 1/4 acre in a city, town, or village; or up to 80 acres elsewhere. If between 1/4 and 1 acre in city, etc., or 80 to 160 acres elsewhere, amount of exemption in limited to $2,500. No homestead may exceed 1 acre in city, etc., or 160 acres elsewhere. This exemption is also found in the State Constitution, and the reference to "Ark. Const. 9-3, 9-4, & 9-5" should also be used.
16-66-218	Real or personal property used as a residence, up to $800 if single or $1,250 if married. Also, $500 of any personal property, if married or head of household; $200 if single (cite "Ark. Const. 9-1; 9-2" also).

PERSONAL PROPERTY (also see §16-66-218 under the homestead section above)

16-66-218	Motor vehicle up to $1,200, and wedding bands provided that any diamonds can't exceed 1/2 carat.
16-66-207	Burial plot up to 5 acres, provided you don't use homestead exemption in section 16-66-218.
Ark. Const.	Clothing of unlimited value; and any personal property of up to $500 if married or head of family, or $200 otherwise. Use reference to "Ark. Const. 9-1 & 9-2."

WAGES

16-66-208	Earned but unpaid wages due for 60 days, but in not less than $25 per week.

PENSIONS

16-66-218	IRA deposits up to $20,000 if deposited over 1 year before filing for bankruptcy.
24-6-223	State police officers.
24-7-715	School employees.
24-10-616	Police officers and firefighters.
24-11-417	Disabled police officers.
24-11-814	Disabled firefighters.

PUBLIC BENEFITS

11-9-110	Worker's compensation.
11-10-109	Unemployment compensation.
16-90-716	Crime victims' compensation, unless you are seeking to discharge a debt for treatment of an injury incurred during the crime.
20-76-430	AFDC, and aid to blind, aged or disabled.

TOOLS OF TRADE

16-66-218	Tools, books and implements of trade to $750.

INSURANCE

16-66-209	Life, health, accident or disability proceeds, whether paid or due (case law limits to $500).
23-71-112	Stipulated insurance premiums.
23-72-114	Mutual assessment life or disability benefits up to $1,000.
23-74-119	Fraternal benefit society benefits.
23-79-131	Life insurance proceeds if beneficiary isn't the insured; life insurance proceeds if policy prohibits proceeds from being used to pay beneficiary's creditors.
23-79-132	Group life insurance.
23-79-133	Disability benefits.
23-79-134	Annuity contract.

MISCELLANEOUS

4-42-502	Business partnership property.
Other	Add any applicable Federal Non-Bankruptcy Exemptions.

NOTE: *The symbol "§" or "§§" stands for section or sections of the statutes or code in your state. It refers to the particular part of the statutes of code listed here to the left of all references. A law librarian can help you.*

CALIFORNIA

West's Annotated California Codes, Civil Procedure, Section 704.710 (Cal. Code Civ. Proc. §704.710). California has two separate systems of exemptions. You must select one, and cannot mix exemptions from the two systems. References are to the California Code of Civil Procedure unless otherwise stated (look for volume marked "Civil Procedure," not just "Civil").

CALIFORNIA (SYSTEM 1)

HOMESTEAD
704.730   Real or personal property occupied at time of filing for bankruptcy, including mobile home, boat, stock cooperative, community apartment, planned development or condominium, up to the following limits: $50,000 if single and not disabled; $75,000 if family and no other member has homestead; $125,000 if 65 or older or if physically or mentally disabled; $125,000 if creditors are seeking to force sale of your home and you are either (a)55 or older, single and earn under $15,000 per year, or (b)55 or older, married and earn under $20,000 per year. Sale proceeds are exempt for up to 6 months after sale. (*)

PERSONAL PROPERTY
704.010   Motor vehicle or insurance if vehicle lost, destroyed or damaged up to $1,900 (*).
704.020   Food, clothing, appliances and furnishings.
704.030   Building materials to repair or improve home up to $2,000 (*).
704.040   Jewelry, heirlooms and art up to $5,000 total (*).
704.050   Health aids.
704.080   Bank deposits from Social Security Administration up to $2,000 for single payee ($3,000 for husband and wife payees); proceeds from exempt property in form of cash or bank deposits.
704.090   Inmates trust funds up to $1,000.
704.140   Personal injury causes of action, and recoveries needed for support.
704.150   Wrongful death causes of action, and recoveries needed for support.
704.200   Burial plot

WAGES
704.070   75% of wages paid within 30 days prior to filing bankruptcy.
704.113   Public employee vacation credits (75% minimum if receiving installment payments).

PENSIONS
704.110   Public retirement benefits.
704.115   Private retirements benefits to extent tax-deferred, including IRA and Keogh.
Gov't. 21201 Public employees.
Gov't. 31452 County employees.
Gov't. 31913 County peace officers.
Gov't. 32210 County fire fighters.

PUBLIC BENEFITS
704.120   Unemployment benefits and union benefits due to labor dispute.
704.160   Workers' compensation.
704.170   AFDC and aid to blind, aged and disabled.
704.180   Relocation benefits.
704.190   Financial aid to students.

TOOLS OF TRADE
704.060   Tools, implements, materials, books, uniforms, instruments, equipment, furnishings, motor vehicle, and vessel up to $5,000, or up to $10,000 if used by both spouses in the same occupation. Can't claim motor vehicle here if already claimed under 704.010.

[CONTINUED ON NEXT PAGE]

INSURANCE

704.100 (**) Matured life insurance benefits needed for support of unlimited value, or unmatured life insurance policy up to $8,000 in value.

704.120 Fraternal unemployment benefits and union benefits in a labor dispute.

704.130 Disability or health benefits.

704.720 Homeowners' insurance proceeds for 6 months after received, up to amount of homestead.

Other Fidelity bonds. Refer to as "Labor 404."

Other Life insurance proceeds if policy prohibits use to pay creditors. Refer to as "Ins. 10132, 10170 & 10171."

MISCELLANEOUS

Corp. 15025 Business partnership property.

Other Add any applicable Federal Non-Bankruptcy Exemptions.

CALIFORNIA (SYSTEM 2) [no doubling of any exemptions]

HOMESTEAD

703.140(b)(1) Real or personal property (e.g., mobile home), including co-op, used as a residence up to $15,000.

PERSONAL PROPERTY

703.140(b)(1) Burial plot up to $15,000, instead of homestead.

703.140(b)(2) Motor vehicle up to $2,400.

703.140(b)(3) Clothing, household goods, appliances, furnishings, animals, books, musical instruments and crops up to $400 per item.

703.140(b)(4) Jewelry up to $1,000.

703.140(b)(5) $15,000 of any property, less any claim for homestead or burial plot.

703.140(b)(5) $800 of any property.

703.140(b)(9) Health aids.

703.140(b)(11) Wrongful death recoveries needed for support.

703.140(b)(11) Personal injury recoveries up to $15,000, not to include pain, suffering or pecuniary loss.

PENSIONS

703.140(b)(10) ERISA-qualified benefits needed for support.

PUBLIC BENEFITS

703.140(b)(10) Unemployment compensation, social security, and public assistance.

703.140(b)(10) Veterans' benefits.

703.140(b)(11) Crime victims' compensation.

TOOLS OF TRADE

703.140(b)(6) Tools, books and implements of trade up to $1,500.

ALIMONY AND CHILD SUPPORT

703.140(b)(10) Alimony and child support needed for support.

INSURANCE

703.140(b)(7) Unmatured life insurance policy, other than credit.

703.140(b)(8) Unmatured life insurance contract accrued interest, dividends, loan, cash or surrender value up to $8,000.

703.140(b)(10) Disability benefits.

703.140(b)(11) Life insurance proceeds needed for support.

Other Fidelity bonds. Refer to as "Labor 404."

MISCELLANEOUS

695.060 Business and professional licenses, except liquor licenses.

Other Add any applicable Federal Non-Bankruptcy Exemptions.

NOTE: *The symbol "§" or "§§" stands for section or sections of the statutes or code in your state. It refers to the particular part of the statutes of code listed here to the left of all references. A law librarian can help you.*

COLORADO

West's Colorado Revised Statutes Annotated, Title 13, Article 54, Section 13-54-102 (C.R.S.A. §13-54-102).

HOMESTEAD
38-41-201 Real property up to $45,000. Property must be occupied at time petition is filed. Sale or insurance proceeds exempt for 1 year. Spouse or child of deceased owner can also qualify.

PERSONAL PROPERTY
13-54-102 Motor vehicles to $3,000 (up to $6,000 if used by elderly or disabled debtor or dependent); clothing to $1,500 for debtor and each dependent; health aids; household goods to $3,000; food and fuel to $600; 1 burial site per person; watches, jewelry, and articles of adornment for debtor and each dependent to $1,000; family pictures and books to $1,500; utility and security deposits; proceeds for damaged exempt property; personal recoveries, unless debt related to the injury.

WAGES
13-54-104 Minimum 75% of earned but unpaid wages, and pension payments. Judge may approve more for low income debtors.

PENSIONS
13-54-102   ERISA-qualified benefits, including IRA's and 401(k)s.
22-64-120   Teachers.
24-51-212   Public employees.
31-30.5-208   Police officers.
31-30-1117   Firefighters.

PUBLIC BENEFITS
8-80-103   Unemployment compensation.
13-54-104   75% of workers' compensation.
13-54-102   Veterans' benefits for veteran, spouse or child if veteran served in war.
13-54-102;24-4.1-114 Crime victims' compensation.
26-2-131   AFDC, aid to blind, aged and disabled.

TOOLS OF TRADE
13-54-102 Stock in trade, supplies, fixtures, maps, machines, tools, electronics, equipment, books, and business materials to $10,000; library of a professional to $3,000; livestock, poultry, or other animals, tractors, farm implements, trucks used in agriculture, harvesting equipment, seed, and agricultural machinery and tools to $25,000.

ALIMONY AND CHILD SUPPORT
13-54-102.5 Child support if recipient doesn't mix with other funds, or if deposited in a separate account for the child's benefit.

INSURANCE
10-7-106   Life insurance proceeds if policy prohibits use to pay creditors.
10-7-205   Group life insurance policy or proceeds.
13-54-104 75% of disability benefits.
10-14-403 Fraternal benefit society benefits.
13-54-102 Life insurance cash surrender value up to $25,000.
38-41-209 Homeowners' insurance proceeds for 1 year after received, up to homestead amount.

MISCELLANEOUS
7-60-125   Business partnership property.
Other   Add any applicable Federal Non-Bankruptcy Exemptions.

NOTE: *The symbol "§" or "§§" stands for section or sections of the statutes or code in your state. It refers to the particular part of the statutes of code listed here to the left of all references. A law librarian can help you.*

CONNECTICUT

Connecticut General Statutes Annotated, Title 52, Section 52-352B (C.G.S.A. §52-352B). Ignore volume and "chapter" numbers; look for "title" and section numbers. Compare federal exemptions.

HOMESTEAD
52-352b   Real property, including mobile or manufactured home, up to $75,000.

PERSONAL PROPERTY
52-352b   Motor vehicle up to $1,500; food, clothing and health aids; appliances, furniture and bedding; wedding and engagement rings; burial plot; residential utility and security deposits for 1 residence; proceeds for damaged exempt property; and $1,000 of any property.

WAGES
52-361a   Minimum 75% of earned but unpaid wages. Judge may approve more for low income debtors.

PENSIONS
5-171;5-192w   State employees.
10-183q   Teachers.
52-352b   ERISA-qualified benefits, but only as to payments received and only to the extent wages are exempt.

PUBLIC BENEFITS
7-446   Municipal employees.
27-140   Vietnam veterans' death benefits.
31-272; 52-352b   Unemployment compensation.
45-48   Probate judges and employees.
52-352b   Workers' compensation; veterans' benefits; social security; wages from earnings incentive programs; AFDC; aid to blind, aged and disabled.
52-352b; 54-213   Crime victims' compensation.

TOOLS OF TRADE
52-352b   Arms, military equipment, uniforms and musical instruments of military personnel; tools, books, instruments and farm animals needed. Farm animals and livestock feed reasonably required, and moneys due from insurance on such property, owned by a farm partnership where at least 50% of the partners are members of the same family.

ALIMONY AND CHILD SUPPORT
52-352b   Alimony and child support, to extent wages are exempt.

INSURANCE
38a-380   Benefits under no-fault insurance law, to extent wages are exempt.
38a-453   Life insurance proceeds, dividends, interest, or cash or surrender value.
38a-454   Life insurance proceeds if policy prohibits use to pay creditors.
38a-636   Fraternal benefit society benefits.
52-352b   Health and disability benefits; disability benefits paid by association for its members; unmatured life insurance policy dividends, interest, or loan value up to $4,000, if you or a person on whom you are dependent is the person whose life is insured.

MISCELLANEOUS
34-63   Business partnership property.

DELAWARE

Delaware Code Annotated, Title 10, Section 4902 (D.C.A. 10 §4902). Ignore volume numbers; look for "title" numbers.

LIMITATION:
10 §4914** Total exemptions (in addition to retirement plans) may not exceed $5,000.

HOMESTEAD
Tenancies by the entirety exempt without limitation as to debts of one spouse. [In re *Hovatter*, 25 B.R. 123 (D. Del. 1982)]; otherwise D.C.A. 10 §4901 says all real estate is subject to execution.

PERSONAL PROPERTY
10 §4902; 10 §4903
Clothing, including jewelry; books; family pictures; piano; leased organs and sewing machines; burial plot; church pew or any seat in public place of worship. Also $500 of any other personal property if head of family (except tools of trade). School books & family library.

WAGES
10 §4913   85% of earned but unpaid wages.

PENSIONS
9 §4316   Kent County employees.
10 §4915   Retirement plans.
11 §8803   Police officers.
16 §6653   Volunteer firefighters.
29 §5503   State employees.

PUBLIC BENEFITS
19 §2355   Workers' compensation.
19 §3374   Unemployment compensation.
31 §513   General assistance; AFDC; aid to aged and disabled.
31 §2309   Aid to blind.

TOOLS OF TRADE
10 §4902   Tools, implements and fixtures, up to $75 in New Castle and Sussex counties, and up to $50 in Kent County.

INSURANCE
12 §1901   Employee life insurance benefits.
18 §2726   Health or disability benefits.
18 §2727   Group life insurance policy or proceeds.
18 §2728   Annuity contract proceeds up to $350 per month.
18 §2729   Life insurance proceeds if policy prohibits use to pay creditors.
18 §6118   Fraternal benefit society benefits.

MISCELLANEOUS
6 §1525   Business partnership property.
Other   Add any applicable Federal Non-Bankruptcy Exemptions.

NOTE: *The symbol "§" or "§§" stands for* section *or* sections *of the statutes or code in your state. It refers to the particular part of the statutes of code listed here to the left of all references. A law librarian can help you.*

DISTRICT OF COLUMBIA

D.C. Code, Title 15, Section 501 (D.C.C. §15-501). Ignore "Chapter" number; look for "title" number. Compare Federal Bankruptcy Exemptions.

HOMESTEAD
Tenancies by the entirety exempt without limit as to debts of one spouse [Estate of Wall, 440 F.2d 215 (D.C.Cir. 1971)].

PERSONAL PROPERTY
15-5-1	Clothing up to $300 (also refer to 15-503); beds, bedding, radios, cooking utensils, stoves, furniture, furnishings, and sewing machines, up to $300 total; books to $400; family pictures; food and fuel to last 3 months.
42-1904.09	Residential condominium deposit.

WAGES
15-503	Non-wage earning, including pensions, for 60 days, up to $200 per month for head of family; or $60 per month otherwise.
16-572	Minimum of 75% of earned but unpaid wages or pension payments.

PENSIONS
1-507; 16-571	DC government employees.
11-1570	Judges.
15-501	ERISA-qualified retirement plans, including IRAs.
38-2001.17, 38-2021.17	DC public school teachers.

PUBLIC BENEFITS
4-215.01	Public assistance.
4-507	Violent crime victims compensation, unless claim is for products, services, or accommodations which are included in the compensation award.
51-118	Unemployment compensation.

TOOLS OF TRADE
15-501	Motor vehicle, cart, wagon or dray, horse or mule harness, up to $500; stock and materials to $200; library, furniture, tools of professional or artist, up to $300.
15-501;15-503	Mechanic's tools, tools of trade or business, up to $200.

INSURANCE
15-503	Other insurance proceeds to $200 per month, for a maximum of 2 months, for head of family; up to $60 per month otherwise.
31-4716.01	Disability benefits.
31-4717	Group life insurance policy or proceeds.
31-5315	Fraternal benefit society benefits.

MISCELLANEOUS
33-105.01	Business partnership property.
Other	Add any applicable Federal Non-Bankruptcy Exemptions.

FLORIDA

Florida Statutes, Chapter 222, Section 222.05 (F.S. §222.05). Ignore volume numbers; look for "chapter" numbers.

HOMESTEAD

222.05   Real or personal property, including mobile or modular home and condominium, to unlimited value. Property cannot exceed 1/2 acre in a municipality, or 160 acres elsewhere. Spouse or child of deceased owner may claim exemption. (Also refer to Florida Constitution, as "Fla. Const. 10-4."). Also, tenancies by the entireties in real property are exempt as to debts of one spouse [In re *Avins*, 19 B.R. 736 (S.D.Fla. 1982)].

PERSONAL PROPERTY

222.25   Motor vehicle up to $1,000; prescribed health aids.

Other   Any personal property up to $1,000 total. (Refer to as "Fla. Const. 10-4")(**).

WAGES

222.11   For head of family, earnings up to $500 a week; also amounts greater than $500 unless debtor has agreed otherwise in writing. For head of family or others, exempt in any event up to amount allowed under the Consumer Credit Protection Act, 15 U.S.C. §1673. Applies to earned but unpaid wages, or wages paid and in a bank account.

PENSIONS

112.215   Government employees' deferred compensation plans.

121.31   State and county officers and employees, and teachers, beginning service on or after 12/1/70; and highway patrol officers.

122.15   County officers and employees beginning service before 12/1/70, unless they elected to transfer to retirement system under Chapter 121.

175.241   Firefighters.

185.25   Police officers.

222.21   Federal government employees' pension payments needed for support and received 3 months before filing bankruptcy. Also, retirement plans under various sections of the Internal Revenue Code, including pension, profit sharing, and stock bonus plans under §401(a); annuity plans [§403(a)]; educational annuities [403(b)]; IRAs [§§408 & 408A]; and employee stock ownership plans [§409]. Also ERISA-qualified benefits.

238.15   Teachers beginning service before 12/1/70, unless they elected to transfer to retirement system under Chapter 121.

PUBLIC BENEFITS

222.201   Public assistance and social security.

222.201; 443.051   Unemployment compensation.

222.201; 744.626   Veterans' benefits.

440.22   Workers' compensation.

769.05   Proceeds for job-related injuries under Chapter 769 relating to hazardous occupations.

960.14   Crime victims' compensation unless seeking to discharge debt for treatment of crime related injury.

ALIMONY AND CHILD SUPPORT

222.201   Alimony and child support needed for support.

INSURANCE

222.13   Death benefits payable to a specific beneficiary.

222.14   Annuity contract proceeds and life insurance cash surrender value.

222.18   Disability or illness benefits.

632.619   Fraternal benefit society benefits.

MISCELLANEOUS

222.22   Funds paid to the Prepaid College Trust Fund or in a Medical Savings Account.

497.413   Funds the debtor may be entitled to from the Florida Department of Banking and Finance Preneed Funeral Contract Consumer Protection Trust Fund.

620.8501   Business partnership property.

Other   Add any applicable Federal Non-Bankruptcy Exemptions.

NOTE: *The symbol "§" or "§§" stands for section or sections of the statutes or code in your state. It refers to the particular part of the statutes of code listed here to the left of all references. A law librarian can help you.*

GEORGIA

Official Code of Georgia Annotated, Title 44, Chapter 13, Section 1 (C.G.A. §44-13-100). [This is not the same set as the "Georgia Code," which is a separate set of books with a completely different numbering system.] Ignore volume numbers; look for "title" and "chapter" numbers.

HOMESTEAD
44-13-100(**)Real or personal property, including coop, used as a residence, up to $10,000. Unused portion may be applied to any other property.

PERSONAL PROPERTY
44-13-100 Motor vehicles up to $3,500; clothing, household goods, appliances, furnishings, books, musical instruments, animals, and crops up to $300 per item and $5,000 total; jewelry up to $500; health aids; lost future earnings recoveries needed for support; personal injury recoveries up to $10,000; wrongful death recoveries needed for support. Also, burial plot in lieu of homestead. Also, any property up to $600 plus any unused homestead amount.

WAGES
18-4-20 Minimum 75% of earned but unpaid wages for private and federal government workers. Judge may approve more for low income debtors.

PENSIONS
18-4-22 ERISA-qualified benefits.
47-2-332 Public employees.
44-13-100 Other pensions needed for support, and IRAs.

PUBLIC BENEFITS
44-13-100 Unemployment compensation, veterans' benefits, social security, crime victims' compensation, and local public assistance.
49-4-35 Old age assistance.
49-4-58 Aid to blind.
49-4-84 Workers' compensation; aid to disabled.

TOOLS OF TRADE
44-13-100 Tools, books and implements of trade up to $1,500.

ALIMONY AND CHILD SUPPORT
44-13-100 Alimony and child support needed for support.

INSURANCE
44-13-100 Unmatured life insurance contract, unmatured life insurance dividends, interest, loan value or cash value up to $2,000 if you or someone you depend on is beneficiary, life insurance proceeds if policy is owned by someone you depend on and is needed for support.
33-15-20 Fraternal benefit society benefits.
33-25-11 Life insurance proceeds, dividends, interest, loan, cash or surrender value, provided that beneficiary is not the insured.
33-28-7 Annuity and endowment contract benefits.
33-27-7 Group insurance.
33-26-5 Industrial life insurance policy owned by someone you depend on for support.
33-29-15 Disability or health benefits up to $250 per month.

MISCELLANEOUS
Other Add any applicable Federal Non-Bankruptcy Exemptions.

HAWAII

Hawaii Revised Statutes Annotated, Chapter 36, Title 651, Section 36-651-92 (H.R.S. §36-651-92). Ignore volume numbers; look for "chapter" and "title" numbers. Compare federal exemptions.

HOMESTEAD
36-651-91;
36-651-92   Up to $30,000 if head of family or over 65; up to $20,000 otherwise. Property can't exceed 1 acre (includes long-term leased land). Sale proceeds are exempt for 6 months after sale. Tenancies by the entirety are exempt without limit as to debts of one spouse [*Security Pacific Bank v. Chang*, 818 F.Supp. (D. Haw. 1993)].

PERSONAL PROPERTY
20-359-104   Down payment for home in state project.
36-651-121   Motor vehicle up to wholesale value of $2,575; clothing; appliances and furnishings needed; books; jewelry, watches, and articles of adornment up to $1,000; proceeds for sold or damaged exempt property (sale proceeds exempt for 6 months after sale); burial plot up to 250 square feet, plus on-site tombstones, monuments and fencing

WAGES
20-353-22   Prisoner's wages held by Dept. of Public Safety.
36-651-121;
36-652-1   Unpaid wages due for services of the past 31 days. If more than 31 days, 95% of first $100, 90% of second $100, and 80% of balance.

PENSIONS
7-88-91;
36-653-3   Public officers and employees.
36-651-124   ERISA-qualified benefits, if deposited more than 3 years before filing.
7-88-169   Police officers and firefighters.

PUBLIC BENEFITS
20-346-33   Public assistance paid by Dept. of Public Safety.
21-383-163   Unemployment compensation.
21-386-57   Workers' compensation.
36-653-4   Unemployment work relief up to $60 per month.

TOOLS OF TRADE
36-651-121   Tools, books, uniforms, implements, instruments, furnishings, fishing boat, nets, motor vehicle and other personal property needed for livelihood.

INSURANCE
24-431:10-231   Disability benefits.
24-431:10-232   Annuity contract or endowment policy proceeds if beneficiary is insured spouse, child or parent.
24-431:10-233   Group life insurance policy or proceeds.
24-431:10-234   Life or health insurance policy for child.
24-431:10-D:112   Life insurance proceeds if policy prohibits use to pay creditors.
24-432:2-403   Fraternal benefit society benefits.

MISCELLANEOUS
23-425-126   Business partnership property.

IDAHO

Idaho Code, Title 55, Section 55-1201 (I.C. §55-1201). Ignore volume number.

HOMESTEAD (*)
55-1003 $50,000. Sale and insurance proceeds are exempt for 1 year (55-1008). If unimproved land, or improved land or mobile home not yet occupied, must file homestead declaration (55-1004).

PERSONAL PROPERTY
11-603   Health aids; burial plot.
11-604   Personal injury and wrongful death recoveries needed for support.
11-605   Motor vehicle up to $3,000; jewelry up to $1,000; clothing, pets, appliances, furnishings, books, musical instruments, family portraits, and sentimental heirlooms up to $500 per item and $5,000 total; 1 firearm up to $500; crops cultivated by the debtor on up to 50 acres (including water rights up to 160 inches) up to $1,000; any tangible personal property up to $800.
11-606   Proceeds for damaged exempt property, for up to 3 months after received.
45-514   Building materials.

WAGES
11-207   Minimum of 75% of earned but unpaid wages and pension payments. Judge may approve more for low income debtors.

PENSIONS
11-604   Payments being received from pensions needed for support, provided payments are not mixed with other money.
11-604A   All employee benefit plans.
50-1517   Police officers.
55-1011   ERISA-qualified benefits.
59-1325   Public employees.
72-1417   Firefighters.

PUBLIC BENEFITS
11-603   Unemployment compensation, social security, veterans' benefits, and federal, state and local public assistance.
56-223   General assistance, AFDC, and aid to blind, aged and disabled.
72-802   Workers' compensation.
72-1020   Crime victims' compensation, unless debt related to injury sustained during the crime.

TOOLS OF TRADE
11-605   Tools, books and implements of trade up to $1,000; arms, uniforms and accoutrements required to be kept by peace officer, national guard or military personnel.

ALIMONY AND CHILD SUPPORT
11-604   Alimony and child support needed for support.

INSURANCE
11-603   Medical or hospital care benefits
11-604;41-1833;
11-605   Unmatured life insurance contract, other than credit life insurance contract; and dividend, interest, or loan value of any unmatured life insurance contract under which the insured is the debtor or the debtor's dependent, up to $5,000.
41-1834   Death and disability benefits; life insurance if insured in not the beneficiary.
41-1830   Life insurance policy if the beneficiary is a married woman.
41-1833   Life insurance proceeds, dividends, interest, loan, cash or surrender value if the insured is not the beneficiary.
41-1835   Group life insurance benefits.
41-1836   Annuity contract proceeds up to $1,250 per month.
41-1930   Life insurance proceeds if policy prohibits use to pay creditors.
41-3218   Fraternal benefit society benefits.

MISCELLANEOUS
53-3-501   Business partnership property.

ILLINOIS

West's Smith-Hurd Illinois Compiled Statutes Annotated, Chapter 735, Act 5, Article 12, Section 5/12-901 (735-5/12-901). Paragraph 12-901 (I.A.S. 110 ¶12-901). Look for "chapter" numbers.

HOMESTEAD (**)
735-5/12-901 Real or personal property, including a farm, lot and buildings, condominium, coop or mobile home, up to $7,500. Spouse or child of deceased owner can claim homestead (735-5/12-902). Sale proceeds up to 1 year (735-5/12-906).

PERSONAL PROPERTY
625-45/3A-7(d) Title certificate for a boat more than 12 feet in length.
735-5/12-1001 Motor vehicle up to $1,200; clothing needed; prescribed health aids; school books; family pictures; bible; personal injury recoveries up to $7,500; wrongful death recoveries needed for support; proceeds from sale of exempt property; any other personal property up to $2,000 (including wages).

WAGES
740-170/4 Minimum 85% of earned but unpaid wages. Judge may approve more for low income debtor.

PENSIONS

40-5/2-154	General assembly members.	50-5/15-185	State university
40-5/3-144; 40-5/5-218	Police officers.	40-5/18-161	Judges.
40-5/4-135; 40-5/6-213	Firefighters.	40-5/19-117	House of correction employees.
40-5/7-217; 40-5/8-244	Municipal employees.		
40-5/9-228	County employees.	40-5/19-218	Public library employees.
40-5/11-223	Civil service employees.	40-5/22-230	Disabled firefighters, and
40-5/12-190	Park employees.		widows and children of
40-5/13-808	Sanitation district employees.		firefighters.
40-5/14-147	State employees.	735-5/12-1006	ERISA-qualified benefits;
50-5/15-185	State university employees.		and public employees.
50-5/16-190; 40-5/17-151	Teachers.		

PUBLIC BENEFITS
305-5/11-3 AFDC; aid to blind, aged and disabled.
820-305-21 Workers' compensation.
820-310/21 Workers' occupational disease compensation.
735-5/12-1001 Veterans' benefits; social security; unemployment compensation; crime victims' compensation; restitution payments for World War II relocation of Japanese Americans and Aleuts under the federal Civil Liberties Act of 1988 and the Aleution and Pribilof Island Restitution Act.

TOOLS OF TRADE
735-5/12-1001 Tools, books and implements of trade up to $750.

ALIMONY AND CHILD SUPPORT
735-5/12-1001 Alimony and child support needed for support.

INSURANCE
215-5/238 Life insurance, annuity or cash value if beneficiary is spouse, child, parent, or other dependent; life insurance proceeds if policy prohibits use to pay creditors.
215-5/299.1a Fraternal benefit society benefits.
735-5/12-907 Homeowners' insurance proceeds for destroyed home, up to $7,500.
735-5/12-1001 Health and disability benefits, life insurance proceeds needed for support, and life insurance policy if beneficiary is spouse or child.

MISCELLANEOUS
805-205/25 Business partnership property.
Other Add any applicable Federal Non-Bankruptcy Exemptions.

INDIANA

West's Annotated Indiana Code, Title 34, Article 2, Chapter 28, Section 1 (A.I.C. §34-2-28-1). Look for "title" numbers.

HOMESTEAD

34-55-10-2 Real or personal property used as a residence up to $7,500 (LIMIT: Homestead plus personal property can't exceed $10,000, not including health aids); tenancies by the entirety exempt without limit unless bankruptcy is seeking to discharge debts incurred by both spouses.

PERSONAL PROPERTY

34-55-10-2 Health aids; up to $4,000 of real or tangible personal property; up to $100 of intangible personal property (except for money owed to you).

WAGES

24-4.5-5-105 Minimum of 75% of earned but unpaid wages. Judge may approve more for low income debtors.

PENSIONS

5-10.3-8-9   Public employees.
10-1-2-9; 36-8-8-17   Police officers, but only as to benefits accruing.
21-6.1-5-17   State teachers.
34-55-10-2   Public or private retirement benefits.
36-8-7-22; 36-8-8-17   Firefighters.
36-8-10-19   Sheriffs, but only benefits accruing.

PUBLIC BENEFITS

16-7-3.6-15 Crime victims' compensation, unless seeking to discharge debt for treatment of crime-related injury.
22-3-2-17   Workers' compensation.
22-4-33-3   Unemployment compensation.

TOOLS OF TRADE

10-2-6-3   National guard arms, uniforms and equipment.

INSURANCE

27-1-12-14 Life insurance policy or proceeds if beneficiary is spouse or dependent.
27-1-12-29 Group life insurance policy.
27-2-5-1   Life insurance proceeds if policy prohibits use to pay creditors.
27-8-3-23   Mutual life or accident policy proceeds.
27-11-6-3   Fraternal benefit society benefits.
34-55-10-2 Medical care saving accounts.

MISCELLANEOUS

23-4-1-25 Business partnership property.
Other   Add any applicable Federal Non-Bankruptcy Exemptions.

NOTE: *The symbol "§" or "§§" stands for section or sections of the statutes or code in your state. It refers to the particular part of the statutes of code listed here to the left of all references. A law librarian can help you.*

IOWA

Iowa Code Annotated, Section 499A.18 (I.C.A. §449A.18). Ignore volume numbers; look for "section" numbers.

HOMESTEAD
499A.18; 561.2; 561.16   Real property or apartment, unlimited in value, but cannot exceed 1/2 acre in a city or town, or 40 acres elsewhere.

PERSONAL PROPERTY
627.6   Motor vehicle, musical instruments and tax refunds up to $5,000 total (but tax refund portion limited to $1,000 of the total); clothing up to $1,000, plus receptacles to hold clothing; household goods, appliances, and furnishings up to $2,000 total; wedding and engagement rings; books, portraits, paintings and pictures up to $1,000; health aids; burial plot up to 1 acre; rifle or musket; shotgun; up to $100 of any other personal property including cash.

WAGES
642.21   Minimum of 75% of earned but unpaid wages and pension payments. Judge may approve more for low income debtors.

PENSIONS
97A-12   Peace officers.
97B-39   Public employees.
410.11   Disabled firefighters and police officers, but only for benefits being received.
411.13   Police officers and firefighters.
627.6   Pensions needed for support, but only as to payments being received, including IRAs.
627.8   Federal government pension, but only as to payments being received.

PUBLIC BENEFITS
627.6   Unemployment compensation, veterans' benefits, social security, AFDC, and local public assistance.
627.13   Workers' compensation.
627.19   Adopted child assistance.

TOOLS OF TRADE
627.6   Non-farming equipment up to $10,000; farming equipment, including livestock and feed, up to $10,000; but not including a car.

ALIMONY AND CHILD SUPPORT
627.6   Alimony and child support needed for support.

INSURANCE
508.32   Life insurance proceeds if policy prohibits use to pay creditors.
509.12   Employee group insurance policy or proceeds.
627.6   Life insurance proceeds up to $10,000, (if acquired within 2 years prior to filing for bankruptcy); and accident, disability, health, illness or life proceeds, dividends, interest, loan, cash or surrender value up to $15,000; if beneficiary is spouse, child or other dependent.

MISCELLANEOUS
123.38   Liquor licenses.
486A.501   Business partnership property.
Other   Add any applicable Federal Non-Bankruptcy Exemptions.

NOTE: *The symbol "§" or "§§" stands for* section *or* sections *of the statutes or code in your state. It refers to the particular part of the statutes of code listed here to the left of all references. A law librarian can help you.*

KANSAS

Kansas Statutes Annotated, Section 60-2301 (K.S.A. §60-2301). Ignore volume numbers; look for "section" numbers. You may find either "*Vernon's* Kansas Statutes Annotated," or "Kansas Statutes Annotated, Official." The most recent law will be in the supplements, which is a pocket part in "*Vernon's*" and a separate soft-cover volume in the "Official." Both have a poor index.

HOMESTEAD
60-2301	Real property or mobile home of unlimited value, but can't exceed 1 acre in a city or town, or 160 acres on a farm. You must occupy or intend to occupy the property at the time you file for bankruptcy. (Also refer to "Const. 15-9").

PERSONAL PROPERTY
60-2304	Motor vehicle up to $20,000 (no limit if equipped or designed for a disabled person); clothing to last 1 year; household equipment and furnishings; food and fuel to last 1 year; jewelry and articles of adornment up to $1,000; burial plot.
16-310	Funeral plan prepayments.

WAGES
60-2310	Minimum of 75% of earned but unpaid wages. Judge may approve more for low income debtor.

PENSIONS
12-5005; 13-14a10	Police officers.
12-5005; 14-10a10	Firefighters.
13-14,102	Elected and appointed officials in cities with populations of between 120,000 and 200,000.
60-2308	Federal government pension needed for support and received within 3 months prior to filing bankruptcy; ERISA-qualified benefits.
72-5526	State school employees.
74-2618	Judges.
74-4923; 74-49,105	Public employees.
74-4989	State highway patrol officers.

PUBLIC BENEFITS
39-717	AFDC; general assistance; social welfare.
44-514	Workers' compensation.
44-718	Unemployment compensation.
74-7313	Crime victims' compensation.

TOOLS OF TRADE
48-245	National guard uniforms, arms and equipment.
60-2304	Equipment, instruments, furniture, books, documents, breeding stock, seed, stock and grain up to $7,500 total.

INSURANCE
40-258	Life insurance proceeds up to $1,000, but only if payable to the decedent's estate.
40-414	Life insurance proceeds or cash value deposited into a bank account; life insurance forfeiture value, only if policy issued over 1 year prior to filing for bankruptcy; fraternal benefit society benefits.
40-414a	Life insurance proceeds if policy prohibits use to pay creditors.

MISCELLANEOUS
41-326	Liquor licenses.
56-325	Business partnership property.
Other	Add any applicable Federal Non-Bankruptcy Exemptions.

NOTE: *The symbol "§" or "§§" stands for* section *or* sections *of the statutes or code in your state. It refers to the particular part of the statutes of code listed here to the left of all references. A law librarian can help you.*

KENTUCKY

Kentucky Revised Statutes. Chapter 427, Section 060 (K.R.S. §427.060). Ignore volume numbers; look for "chapter" numbers.

HOMESTEAD
427.060   Real or personal property used as a family residence up to $5,000. Sale proceeds are also exempt.

PERSONAL PROPERTY
304.39-260 Reparation benefits received and medical expenses paid under motor vehicle reparation law.
427.010   Motor vehicle up to $2,500; health aids; clothing, furniture, jewelry and articles of adornment up to $3,000 total.
427.060   Burial plot up to $5,000, in lieu of homestead.
427.150   Lost earnings payments needed for support; wrongful death recoveries for person you depended upon for support; personal injury recoveries up to $7,500, but not including pain, suffering or pecuniary loss.
427.160 $1,000 of any property.

WAGES
427.101   Minimum of 75% of earned but unpaid wages. Judge may approve more for low income debtor.

PENSIONS
61.690   State employees.
67A.350   Urban county government employees.
67A.620;95.878;
427.120;427.125   Police officers and firefighters.
161.700   Teachers.
427.150   Other pensions needed for support, including IRAs.

PUBLIC BENEFITS
205.220   AFDC; aid to blind, aged and disabled.
341.470   Unemployment compensation.
342.180   Workers' compensation.
427.110   Cooperative life or casualty insurance benefits; fraternal benefit society benefits.
427.150   Crime victims' compensation.

TOOLS OF TRADE
427.010   Farmer's tools, equipment, livestock and poultry up to $3,000.
427.030   Non-farmer's tools up to $300; motor vehicle of mechanic, mechanical or electrical equipment servicer, minister, attorney, physician, surgeon, dentist, veterinarian or chiropractor up to $2,500.
427.040   Library, office equipment, instruments and furnishings of a minister, attorney, physician, surgeon, dentist, veterinarian or chiropractor up to $1,000.

ALIMONY AND CHILD SUPPORT
427.150   Alimony and child support needed for support.

INSURANCE
304.14-300 Life insurance proceeds or cash value if beneficiary is not the insured.
304.14-310 Health or disability benefits.
304.14-320 Group life insurance proceeds.
304.14-330 Annuity contract proceeds up to $350 per month.
304.14-340 Life insurance policy if the beneficiary is a married woman.
304.14-350 Life insurance proceeds if policy prohibits use to pay creditors.

MISCELLANEOUS
362.270   Business partnership property.
Other   Add any applicable Federal Non-Bankruptcy Exemptions.

NOTE: *The symbol "§" or "§§" stands for* section *or* sections *of the statutes or code in your state. It refers to the particular part of the statutes of code listed here to the left of all references. A law librarian can help you.*

LOUISIANA

West's LSA Revised Statutes, Title 20, Section 1 (L.R.S.A. §20:1). Ignore volume numbers; look for "section" numbers. Also, be sure to use the volumes marked "Revised Statutes," except for the item marked "Civil 223" under PERSONAL PROPERTY, which will be found in a volume marked "*West's* LSA Civil Code."

HOMESTEAD
20:1   Up to $25,000, but cannot exceed 5 acres if the residence in a municipality, or 200 acres if not located in a municipality. As to obligations arising directly as a result of a catastrophic or terminal illness or injury, exemption is the full value of the based on value one year before seizure. Spouse or child of deceased owner, or spouse obtaining home in divorce may also claim the exemption. (*)

PERSONAL PROPERTY
8:313   Cemetery plot and monuments.
13:3881   Living room, dining room and bedroom furniture; clothing; chinaware, glassware, utensils, and silverware (but not sterling); refrigerator, freezer, stove, washer and dryer; bedding and linens; family portraits; musical instruments; heating and cooling equipment; pressing irons and sewing machine; arms and military accoutrements; poultry, fowl and 1 cow; engagement and wedding rings up to $5,000; and equipment needed for therapy. Also, property of a minor child (also cite as "Civil 223").

WAGES
13:3881   Minimum of 75% of earned but unpaid wages. Judge may approve more for low income debtor.

PENSIONS
13:3881   ERISA-qualified benefit contributions, if deposited more than 1 year before filing.
20:33   Gratuitous payments to employee or heirs, whenever paid.

PUBLIC BENEFITS
23:1205   Workers' compensation.
23:1693   Unemployment compensation.
46:111   AFDC; aid to blind, aged and disabled.
46:1811   Crime victims' compensation.

TOOLS OF TRADE
13:3881   Tools, books, instruments, non-luxury car, pickup truck (under 3 tons), and utility trailer needed for work.

INSURANCE
22:558   Fraternal benefit society benefits.
22:646   Health, accident or disability proceeds, dividends, interest, loan, cash or surrender value.
22:647   Life insurance proceeds, dividends, interest, loan, cash or surrender value, if policy issued within 9 months of filing, up to $35,000.
22:649   Group insurance policies or proceeds.

MISCELLANEOUS
Other   Add any applicable Federal Non-Bankruptcy Exemptions.

NOTE: *The symbol "§" or "§§" stands for section or sections of the statutes or code in your state. It refers to the particular part of the statutes of code listed here to the left of all references. A law librarian can help you.*

MAINE

Maine Revised Statutes Annotated, Title 14, Section 4422 (14 M.R.S.A. §4422). Ignore volume numbers; look for "title" numbers.

HOMESTEAD (**)
14-4422 $12,500 (up to $60,000 if over 60 or disabled). Includes co-op and property owned by the debtor but used as a residence by a dependent of the debtor. Proceeds for 6 months (must be reinvested in new homestead within 6 months).

PERSONAL PROPERTY
9-A-5-103   Balance due on repossessed goods, provided total amount financed is not more than $2,000.

14-4422   Motor vehicle up to $2,500; cooking stove; furnaces and stoves for heat; food to last 6 months; fuel not to exceed 5 tons of coal, 1,000 gallons of oil, or 10 cords of wood; health aids; 1 wedding ring & 1 engagement ring; other jewelry up to $750; up to $200 per item for each of the following: household goods & furnishings, clothing, appliances, books, animals, crops, and musical instruments; lost earnings payments needed for support; feed, seed, fertilizer, tools and equipment to raise and harvest food for 1 season; wrongful death recoveries needed for support; personal injury recoveries up to $12,500, not including pain and suffering; $400 of any property. Burial plot for the debtor or a dependent of the debtor, in lieu of homestead exemption.

37-B-262   Military arms, clothes and equipment.

PENSIONS
3-703	Legislators.	5-17054	State employees.
4-1203	Judges.	14-4422	ERISA-qualified benefits.

PUBLIC BENEFITS
14-4422   Unemployment compensation, veterans' benefits, social security, and crime victims' compensation.

22-3753   AFDC

39-67   Workers' compensation.

TOOLS OF TRADE
14-4422   Books, materials and stock up to $5,000; 1 of each type of farm implement necessary to raise and harvest crops; 1 boat not to exceed 5 tons used in commercial fishing.

ALIMONY AND CHILD SUPPORT
14-4422   Alimony and child support needed for support.

INSURANCE
14-4422   Unmatured life insurance policy; life insurance policy, dividends, interest, or loan value for person you depended upon up to $4,000.

24-A-2428   Life, annuity, accident or endowment policy, proceeds, dividends, interest, loan, cash or surrender value.

24-A-2429   Disability or health insurance proceeds, dividends, interest, loan, cash or surrender value.

24-A-2430   Group life or health policy or proceeds.

24-A-2431   Annuity proceeds up to $450 per month.

24-A-4118   Fraternal benefit society benefits.

MISCELLANEOUS
14-4422   Unused homestead to $6,000 total for tools of trade, personal injury recoveries, or household goods & furnishings, clothing, appliances, books, animals, crops, and musical instruments.

31-305   Business partnership property.

Other   Add any applicable Federal Non-Bankruptcy Exemptions.

NOTE: *The symbol "§" or "§§" stands for* section *or* sections *of the statutes or code in your state. It refers to the particular part of the statutes of code listed here to the left of all references. A law librarian can help you.*

MARYLAND

References with numbers only are to Annotated Code of Maryland, Article 23, Section 164 (A.C.M. §23-164). Other references are to specific volumes, which have the title on the book. Example: "A.C.M. Courts and Judicial Procedure §11-504 (Ct. & Jud. Proc. 11-504)," or "A.C.M. Corporations §9-502 (Corp. 9-502)."

HOMESTEAD

Tenancies by the entirety to unlimited amount as to debts of one spouse [In re *Sefren*, 41 B.R. 747 (D. Md. 1984)].

PERSONAL PROPERTY

Ct.&Jud.Proc.11-504	Clothing, household goods & furnishings, appliances, books and pets up to $500 total; health aids; cash or property up to $3,000; lost future earnings recoveries.
23-164	Burial plot.

WAGES

Comm.15-601.1	Earned but unpaid wages are exempt as follows: in Kent, Caroline and Queen Anne's of Worcester counties, the greater of 75% of actual wages or 30% of the federal minimum wage; in all other counties, the greater of 75% or $145 per week.

PENSIONS

73B-17;73B-125	State employees.
73B-49	Deceased Baltimore police officers, but only as to benefits accruing.
73B-96;73B-152	Teachers.
88B-60	State police.
Ct. & Jud. Proc. 11-504	ERISA-qualified benefits, except IRAs.

PUBLIC BENEFITS

26A-13	Crime victims' compensation.
88A-73	AFDC; general assistance.
95A-16	Unemployment compensation.
101-50	Workers' compensation.

TOOLS OF TRADE

Ct.&Jud.Proc.11-504	Tools, books, instruments, appliances and clothing needed for work (but can't include car), up to $2,500.

INSURANCE

48A-328,Estates and Trusts 8-115	Fraternal benefit society benefits.
48A-385,Estates and Trusts 8-115	Life insurance or annuity contract proceeds, dividends, interest, loan, cash or surrender value if beneficiary is a dependent of the insured.
Comm.15-601.1	Medical benefits deducted from wages.
Ct.&Jud.Proc.11-504	Disability or health benefits.

MISCELLANEOUS

Corp. 9-502	Business partnership property.
Other	Add any applicable Federal Non-Bankruptcy Exemptions.

NOTE: *The symbol "§" or "§§" stands for section or sections of the statutes or code in your state. It refers to the particular part of the statutes of code listed here to the left of all references. A law librarian can help you.*

MASSACHUSETTS

Annotated Laws of Massachusetts, Chapter 188, Section 1 (A.L.M. §188-1). Compare Federal Bankruptcy Exemptions.

HOMESTEAD

188-1; 188-1A	$100,000; if over 65 or disabled then $200,000. Some tenancies by the entirety are exempt without limit. Must record homestead declaration before filing bankruptcy. Must occupy or intend to occupy the property at the time of filing for bankruptcy. Spouse or child of deceased owner may claim the exemption.(*)
209-1	Tenancies by the entirety exempt as against debts for non-necessities.

PERSONAL PROPERTY

79-6A	Moving expenses for eminent domain (that is, if the government took your property).
235-34	Motor vehicle up to $750; furniture up to $3,000; clothing needed; beds and bedding; heating unit; books up to $200 total; cash up to $200 per month for rent, in lieu of homestead; cash for fuel, heat, water or electricity up to $75 per month; bank deposits to $125; cash for food or food to $300; sewing machine to $200; burial plots and tombs; church pew; 2 cows, 2 swine, 12 sheep and 4 tons of hay. Co-op shares up to $100.
246-28A	Bank, credit union or trust company deposits up to $500 total.

WAGES

246-28	Earned but unpaid wages up to $125 per week.

PENSIONS

32-19	Public employees.
32-41	Private retirement benefits.
168-41; 168-44	Savings bank employees.
235-34A; 246-28	ERISA-qualified benefits.

PUBLIC BENEFITS

115-5	Veterans' benefits.	152-47	Workers' compensation.
118-10	AFDC	235-34	Aid to aged and disabled.
151A-36	Unemployment compensation.		

TOOLS OF TRADE

235-34	Tools, implements and fixtures up to $500 total; materials you designed and procured up to $500; boats, nets and fishing tackle of fisherman up to $500; arms, uniforms and accoutrements you are required to keep.

INSURANCE

175-110A	Disability benefits up to $400 per week.
175-119A	Life insurance proceeds if policy prohibits use to pay creditors.
175-125	Life insurance annuity contract which states it is exempt; life or endowment policy, proceeds, dividends, interest, loan, cash or surrender value.
175-126	Life insurance policy if beneficiary is a married woman.
175-132C	Group annuity policy or proceeds.
175-135	Group life insurance policy.
175F-15	Medical malpractice self-insurance.
176-22	Fraternal benefit society benefits.

MISCELLANEOUS

108A-25	Business partnership property.
Other	Add any applicable Federal Non-Bankruptcy Exemptions.

MICHIGAN

Michigan Compiled Laws Annotated, Section 600.6023 (M.C.L.A. §600.6023). [**NOTE:** *You may come across an old set of books titled* Michigan Statutes Annotated *(abbreviated M.S.A.), which uses a different numbering system. This set is being phased out, and new laws are not being assigned an M.S.A. number. If this is the only set you can find, it will have a volume of Tables which will cross-reference the M.C.L.A. and M.S.A. numbers.*] Compare Federal Bankruptcy Exemptions.

HOMESTEAD

600.6023	Real property, including condominium, up to $3,500; but may not exceed 1 lot in a city, town, or village, or 40 acres elsewhere Spouse or child of deceased owner may claim the exemption. Tenancies by the entirety are exempt without limit as to debts of one spouse [*SNB Bank & Trust* v. *Kensey,* 378 NW2d 594 (Mich. App. 1985)].

PERSONAL PROPERTY

128.112	Burial plots.
600.6023	Clothing; household goods, furniture, appliances, utensils and books up to $1,000 total; food and fuel to last 6 months if head of household; building and loan association shares up to $1,000 par value, in lieu of homestead exemption; family pictures; church pew, slip or seat; 2 cows, 5 swine, 10 sheep, 5 roosters, 100 hens, and hay and grain to last 6 months if head of household.

WAGES

600.5311	60% of earned but unpaid wages for head of household; 40% for others; subject to following minimums: $15 per week plus $2 per week for each dependent other than spouse for head of household; $10 per week for others.

PENSIONS

38.40	State employees.	38.1057	Legislators.
38.559	Police officers and firefighters.	38.1346	Public school employees.
38.826	Judges.	600.6023	IRAs, to extent tax-deferred; ERISA-qualified benefits.
38.927	Probate judges.		

PUBLIC BENEFITS

18.362	Crime victims' compensation.
35.926	Veterans' benefits for WWII veterans.
35.977	Korean War veterans' benefits.
35.1027	Vietnam veterans' benefits.
330.1158a	AFDC.
400.63	Social welfare benefits.
418.821	Workers' compensation.
421.30	Unemployment compensation.

TOOLS OF TRADE

600.6023	Tools, implements, materials, stock, apparatus, motor vehicle, horse, team and harness up to $1,000 total; arms and accoutrements you are required to keep.

INSURANCE

500.2207	Life insurance proceeds, dividends, interest, loan, cash or surrender value; life or endowment proceeds if beneficiary is spouse or child of insured.
500.2209	Life insurance proceeds up to $300 per year if the beneficiary is a married woman or a husband.
500.4054	Life, annuity or endowment proceeds if policy or contract prohibits use to pay creditors.
500.8046	Fraternal benefit society benefits.
600.6023	Disability, mutual life or health benefits.

MISCELLANEOUS

449.25	Business partnership property

Other   Add any applicable Federal Non-Bankruptcy Exemptions.

NOTE: *The symbol "§" or "§§" stands for* section *or* sections *of the statutes or code in your state. It refers to the particular part of the statutes of code listed here to the left of all references. A law librarian can help you.*

MINNESOTA

Minnesota Statutes Annotated, Section 510.01 (M.S.A. §510.01). Ignore volume numbers; look for "section" numbers. [NOTE: *Some courts have held "unlimited" exemptions invalid as state constitution only allows for "reasonable" exemptions; see* In re Tveten, *402 NW2d 551 (Minn. 1987).*] Be sure to check Cumulative Annual Pocket Part as amounts are required to be adjusted periodically. Compare Federal Bankruptcy Exemptions.

HOMESTEAD
510.01;510.02; 550.37   Real property, mobile or manufacturer home up to $200,000 ($500,000 if used primarily for agriculture), but cannot exceed 1/2 acre in "the laid out or platted portion of" a city or 160 acres elsewhere. Sale and insurance proceeds for 1 year.

PERSONAL PROPERTY
550.37   Motor vehicle up to $2,000 ($20,000 if modified for disability at a cost of at least $1,500); clothing, including watch; furniture, appliances, radio, TV, and phonographs, up to $4,500 total; food and utensils; books and musical instruments; burial plot; church pew or seat; proceeds for damaged or destroyed exempt property; personal injury lost earnings, and wrongful death recoveries.

WAGES
550.37   Wages deposited into bank accounts for 20 days after deposit; earned but unpaid wages paid within 6 months of returning to work if you previously received welfare; wages of released inmates paid received within 6 months of release.

571.55   Minimum of 75% of earned but unpaid wages. Judge may approve more for low income debtor.

550.37   Earnings of a minor child.

PENSIONS
181B.16	Private retirement benefits accruing.		550.37	ERISA-qualified benefits, including IRAs, needed for support, up to $51,000 present value.
352.15	State employees.			
352B.071	State troopers.			
353.15	Public employees.			
354.10;354A.11	Teachers.			

PUBLIC BENEFITS
176.175   Workers' compensation.
268.17   Unemployment compensation.
550.37   AFDC, supplemental security income (SSI), general assistance, supplemental assistance.
550.38   Veterans' benefits.
611A.60   Crime victims' compensation.

TOOLS OF TRADE
550.37   Tools, library, furniture, machines, instruments, implements and stock in trade up to $5,000; Farm machines, implements, livestock, produce and crops of farmers up to $13,000. (Total of these cannot exceed $13,000.) Teaching materials of a school teacher, including books and chemical apparatus, of unlimited value and not subject to $13,000 limit.

INSURANCE
61A.04   Life insurance proceeds if policy prohibits use to pay creditors.
61A.12   Life insurance or endowment proceeds, dividends, interest, loan, cash or surrender value if the insured is not the beneficiary.
64B.18   Fraternal benefit society benefits.
550.37   Life insurance proceeds if beneficiary is spouse or child, up to $20,000 plus additional $5,000 per dependent; unmatured life insurance contract dividends, interest, loan, cash, or surrender value if insured is the debtor or someone the debtor depends upon up to $4,000; police, fire, or beneficiary association benefits.
550.39   Accident or disability proceeds.

MISCELLANEOUS
323.24   Business partnership property.
Other   Add any applicable Federal Non-Bankruptcy Exemptions.

NOTE: *The symbol "§" or "§§" stands for* section *or* sections *of the statutes or code in your state. It refers to the particular part of the statutes of code listed here to the left of all references. A law librarian can help you.*

MISSISSIPPI

Mississippi Code 1972 Annotated, Title 85, Section 85-3-21 (M.C. §85-3-21).

HOMESTEAD

85-3-21	$75,000, but cannot exceed 160 acres. Must occupy at time of filing bankruptcy, unless you are widowed or over 60 and married or widowed. Sale proceeds are also exempt. 85-3-23.

PERSONAL PROPERTY

85-3-1	Tangible personal property of any kind up to $10,000; proceeds from exempt property.
85-3-17	Personal injury judgments up to $10,000.

WAGES

85-3-4	Earned but unpaid wages owed for 30 days, 75% after 30 days.

PENSIONS

21-29-257	Police officers and firefighters.
25-11-129	Public employees retirement and disability benefits.
25-11-201-23	Teachers.
25-13-31	Highway patrol officers.
25-14-5	State employees.
71-1-43	Private retirement benefits.
85-3-1	IRAs, Keoghs, and ERISA-qualified benefits, if deposited more than 1 year before filing.

PUBLIC BENEFITS

25-11-129	Social security.
43-3-71	Assistance to blind.
43-9-19	Assistance to aged.
43-29-15	Assistance to disabled.
71-3-43	Workers' compensation.
71-5-539	Unemployment compensation.
99-41-23	Crime victims' compensation.

INSURANCE

83-7-5	Life insurance proceeds if policy prohibits use to pay creditors.
83-29-39	Fraternal benefit society benefits.
85-3-1	Disability benefits.
85-3-11	Life insurance policy or proceeds up to $50,000.
85-3-13	Life insurance proceeds if beneficiary is the decedent's estate, up to $5,000.
85-3-23	Homeowners' insurance proceeds up to $75,000.

MISCELLANEOUS

79-12-49	Business partnership property.
Other	Add any applicable Federal Non-Bankruptcy Exemptions.

NOTE: *The symbol "§" or "§§" stands for* section *or* sections *of the statutes or code in your state. It refers to the particular part of the statutes of code listed here to the left of all references. A law librarian can help you.*

MISSOURI

Vernon's Annotated Missouri Statutes, Chapter 513, Section 513.430 (A.M.S. §513.430). Ignore volume numbers; look for "section" numbers.

HOMESTEAD

513.430;	
513.475	Real property up to $8,000, or mobile home up to $1,000. Tenancies by the entirety are exempt without limit as to debts of one spouse [In re *Anderson*, 12 B.R. 483 (W.D. Mo. 1981)].(*)

PERSONAL PROPERTY

214.190	Burial grounds up to $100 or 1 acre.
513.430	Motor vehicle up to $1,000; clothing, household goods, appliances, furnishings, books, animals, musical instruments and crops up to $1,000 total; health aids; jewelry up to $500; wrongful death recoveries for a person you depended upon.
513.430;	
513.440	Any property up to $1,250 plus $250 per child for head of family; up to $400 for others.
Other	Personal injury causes of action. Refer to as: "In re *Mitchell*, 73 B.R. 93".

WAGES

513.470	Wages of a servant or common laborer up to $90.
525.030	Minimum of 75% of earned but unpaid wages. Judge may approve more for low income debtor. 90% for head of family.

PENSIONS

70.695	Public officers and employees.
71.207	Employees of cities with more than 100,000 population.
86.190;86.353; 86.493;86.780	Police department employees.
87.090;87.365; 87.485	Firefighters.
104.250	Highway and transportation employees.
104.540	State employees.
169.090	Teachers.
513.430	ERISA-qualified benefits needed for support; life insurance dividends, loan value, or interest, up to $5,000, if bought more than 6 months before filing.

PUBLIC BENEFITS

287.260	Workers' compensation.
288.380; 513.430	Unemployment compensation.
513.430	Social security, veterans' benefits, and AFDC.

TOOLS OF TRADE

513.430	Tools, books and implements to $2,000.

ALIMONY AND CHILD SUPPORT

513.430	Alimony and child support up to $500 per month.

INSURANCE

376.530; 376.560	Life insurance proceeds if policy owned by woman insuring her husband.
376.550	Life insurance proceeds if policy owned by an unmarried woman and beneficiary is her father or brother.
377.090	Fraternal benefit society benefits, up to $5,000, if bought more than 6 months before filing.
377.330	Assessment or stipulated premium proceeds.
513.430	Death, disability or illness benefits needed for support; unmatured life insurance policy.

MISCELLANEOUS

358.250	Business partnership property.
Other	Add any applicable Federal Non-Bankruptcy Exemptions.

WILDERMUTH

NOTE: *The symbol "§" or "§§" stands for section or sections of the statutes or code in your state. It refers to the particular part of the statutes of code listed here to the left of all references. A law librarian can help you.*

MONTANA

Montana Code Annotated, Title 70, Chapter 32, Section 70-32-101 (M.C.A. §70-32-101). Ignore volume numbers; look for "title" numbers.

HOMESTEAD
70-32-101; 70-32-104;

70-32-201   Real property or mobile home up to $100,000. Must occupy at time of filing for bankruptcy, and must record a homestead declaration before filing (70-32-106 & 107). Proceeds for 18 months (70-32-216).

PERSONAL PROPERTY
25-13-608   Health aids; burial plot.

25-13-609   Motor vehicle up to $2,500; clothing, household goods and furnishings, appliances, jewelry, books, animals and feed, musical instruments, firearms, sporting goods, and crops up to $600 per item and $4,500 total.

25-13-610   Proceeds for damaged or lost exempt property for 6 months after receipt.

35-15-404   Cooperative association shares up to $500 value.

WAGES
25-13-614   Minimum of 75% of earned but unpaid wages. Judge may approve more for low income debtor.

PENSIONS

19-3-105	Public employees.	19-9-1006;19-10-504	Police officers.
19-4-706	Teachers.	19-11-612;19-13-1004	Firefighters.
19-5-704	Judges.	19-21-212	University system employees.
19-6-705	Highway patrol officers.	31-2-106	ERISA-qualified benefits in excess of
19-7-705	Sheriffs.		15% of annual income, if deposited at
19-8-805	Game wardens.		least 1 year before filing.

PUBLIC BENEFITS
25-13-608   Social security, veterans', & local public assistance benefits.

39-71-743   Workers' compensation.

39-73-110   Silicosis benefits.

39-51-3105   Unemployment compensation.

53-2-607   AFDC, aid to aged and disabled, vocational rehabilitation to the blind, subsidized adoption payments.

53-9-129   Crime victims' compensation.

TOOLS OF TRADE
25-13-609   Tools, books and instruments of trade up to $3,000.

25-13-613   Arms, uniforms and accoutrements needed to carry out government functions.

ALIMONY AND CHILD SUPPORT
25-13-608   Alimony and child support.

INSURANCE
25-13-608; 33-15-513   Disability or illness proceeds, benefits, dividends, interest, loan, cash or surrender value, and medical or hospital benefits.

25-13-609   Unmatured life insurance contracts up to $4,000.

33-7-511   Fraternal benefit society benefits.

33-15-511   Life insurance proceeds, dividends, interest, loan, cash or surrender value.

33-15-512   Group life insurance policy or proceeds.

33-15-514   Annuity contract proceeds up to $350 per month.

33-20-120   Life insurance proceeds if policy prohibits use to pay creditors.

80-2-245   Hail insurance benefits.

MISCELLANEOUS
35-10-508   Business partnership property.

Other   Add any applicable Federal Non-Bankruptcy Exemptions.

NEBRASKA

Revised Statutes of Nebraska, Chapter 40, Section 40-101 (R.S.N. §40-101). Ignore volume numbers; look for "chapter" numbers.

HOMESTEAD
40-101 $12,500, but cannot exceed 2 lots in a city or 160 acres elsewhere. Sale proceeds are exempt for 6 months (40-113).

PERSONAL PROPERTY
12-511   Perpetual care funds.
12-517   Burial plot.
12-605   Tombs, crypts, lots, niches and vaults.
25-1552 $2,500 of any property except wages, in lieu of homestead.
25-1556   Personal possessions; clothing needed; furniture and kitchen utensils up to $1,500; food and fuel to last 6 months.
25-1563   Recovery for personal injuries.

WAGES
25-1558   Minimum of 85% of earned but unpaid wages or pension payments for head of family; 75% for others. Judge may approve more for low income debtor.

PENSIONS
23-2322   County employees.
25-1559   Military disability benefits up to $2,000.
25-1563-01 ERISA-qualified benefits needed for support.
79-1060;
79-1552   School employees.
84-1324   State employees.

PUBLIC BENEFITS
48-149   Workers' compensation.
48-647   Unemployment compensation.
68-1013   AFDC; aid to blind, aged and disabled.

TOOLS OF TRADE
25-1556   Tools or equipment up to $2,000. (**) (Can include motor vehicle used for work or to commute to and from workplace.)

INSURANCE
44-371   Life insurance or annuity contract proceeds up to $10,000 loan value.
44-754   Disability benefits to $200 per month.
44-1089   Fraternal benefit society benefits up to loan value of $10,000.

MISCELLANEOUS
67-427   Business partnership property.
Other   Add any applicable Federal Non-Bankruptcy Exemptions.

NEVADA

Nevada Revised Statutes Annotated, Chapter 21, Section 21.090 (N.R.S.A. §21.090(m)). Ignore volume numbers; look for "chapter" numbers.

HOMESTEAD (*)

21.090(m); 115.010	Real property or mobile home up to $125,000. Must record a homestead declaration before filing for bankruptcy (115.020).

PERSONAL PROPERTY

21.090	Motor vehicle up to $1,500 (no limit if equipped for the disabled); household goods, furniture, home and yard equipment up to $3,000 total; books up to $1,500 total; pictures and keepsakes; health aids; 1 gun.
21.100	Metal-bearing ores, geological specimens, paleontological remains or art curiosities (must be arranged, classified, catalogued, and numbered in reference books).
452.550	Burial plot purchase money held in trust.
689.700	Funeral service contract money held in trust.

WAGES

21.090	Minimum of 75% of earned but unpaid wages. Judge may approve more for low income debtor.

PENSIONS

21.090	Up to $500,000 in an IRA, or retirement plans under various sections of the Internal Revenue Code, including simplified employee pension plan under 26 U.S.C. § 408, cash or deferred arrangement plan, or a trust forming part of a stock bonus, pension or profit-sharing plan under 26 U.S.C. §§ 401 et seq.).
286.670	Public employees.

PUBLIC BENEFITS

422.291	AFDC; aid to blind, aged and disabled.
612.710	Unemployment compensation.
615.270	Vocational rehabilitation benefits.
616.550	Industrial insurance (worker's compensation).

TOOLS OF TRADE

21.090	Tools, materials, library, equipment and supplies up to $4,500; farm trucks, equipment, tools, stock and seed up to $4,500; cabin or dwelling of a miner or prospector, cars, implements and appliances for mining and a mining claim you work up to $4,500; arms, uniforms and accoutrements you are required to keep.

INSURANCE

21.090	Life insurance policy or proceeds if premiums don't exceed $1,000 per year.
687B.260	Life insurance proceeds if you are not insured.
687B.270	Health insurance proceeds, dividends, interest, loan, cash or surrender value.
687B.280	Group life or health policy or proceeds.
687B.290	Annuity contract proceeds up to $350 per month.
695A.220	Fraternal benefit society benefits.

MISCELLANEOUS

87.250	Business partnership property.
Other	Add any applicable Federal Non-Bankruptcy Exemptions.

NEW HAMPSHIRE

New Hampshire Revised Statutes Annotated, Chapter 480, Section 480:1 (N.H.R.S.A. §480:1). Ignore "title" numbers; look for "chapter" numbers.

HOMESTEAD
480:1   Real property, or manufactured home, up to $30,000.

PERSONAL PROPERTY
511:2   (1) clothing; (2) beds, bedsteads, and bedding; (3) furniture up to $3,500; (4) one refrigerator, cooking stove, and heating stove, and utensils for each; (5) sewing machine; (6) provisions and fuel up to $400; (7) books up to $800; (8) 1 hog and 1 pig, or pork if already slaughtered; (9) 6 sheep and their fleeces; (10) 1 cow, 1 yoke of oxen or a horse (if needed for farming, etc.), and hay up to 4 tons; (11) domestic fowls up to $300; (12) church pew; (13) automobile up to $4,000; (14) jewelry up to $500; and (15) any property up to $1,000. Also up to $7,000 in any property for any unused amounts allowed for items (3), (6), (7), (13), (14), and tools of trade.

512:21   Proceeds for lost or destroyed exempt property.

WAGES
512:21   Earned but unpaid wages of debtor and spouse (Judge determines amount exempt based on percent of federal minimum wage, so claim all); jury and witness fees; wages of a minor child.

PENSIONS
100A:26	Public employees.	103:18	Police officers.
102:23	Firefighters.	512:21	Federally created pensions accruing.

PUBLIC BENEFITS
167:25   AFDC; aid to blind, aged and disabled.
281A:52   Workers' compensation.
282A:159   Unemployment compensation.

TOOLS OF TRADE
511:2   Tools of trade up to $5,000; arms, uniforms and equipment of a military member; 1 yoke of oxen or horse needed for farming or teaming.

ALIMONY AND CHILD SUPPORT
161C:11   Child support only.

INSURANCE
402:69   Firefighters' aid insurance.
408:1   Life insurance or endowment proceeds if beneficiary is a married woman.
408:2   Life insurance or endowment proceeds if you are not the insured.
418:24   Fraternal benefit society benefits.
512:21   Homeowners' insurance proceeds up to $5,000.

MISCELLANEOUS
304A:25   Business partnership property.
Other   Add any applicable Federal Non-Bankruptcy Exemptions.

NOTE: *The symbol "§" or "§§" stands for section or sections of the statutes or code in your state. It refers to the particular part of the statutes of code listed here to the left of all references. A law librarian can help you.*

NEW JERSEY

New Jersey Statutes Annotated, Title 2A, Chapter 17, Section 2A-17-19 (N.J.S.A. §2A:17-19). The spine of these volumes will be marked "NJSA." Compare Federal Bankruptcy Exemptions.

PERSONAL PROPERTY

2A:17-19	Clothing; goods, personal property and stock or interest in corporations up to $1,000 total.
2A:26-4	Household good and furniture up to $1,000.
8A:5-10	Burial plots.

WAGES

2A:17-56	90% of earned but unpaid wages if your income is less than $7,500; otherwise judge may exempt less.
38A:4-8	Military personnel wages and allowances.

PENSIONS

A:057.6	Civil defense workers.
18A:66-51	Teachers.
18A:66-116	School district employees.
43:6A-41	Judges.
43:7-13	Prison employees.
43:8A-20	Alcohol beverage control officers.
43:10-57; 43:10-105	County employees.
43-13-9	ERISA-qualified benefits.
43:13-44	Municipal employees.
43:15A-55	Public employees.
43:16-7; 43:16A-17	Police officers, firefighters and traffic officers.
43:18-12	City boards of health employees.
43:19-17	Street and water department employees.
53:5A-45	State police.

PUBLIC BENEFITS

34:15-29	Workers' compensation.
43:21-53	Unemployment compensation.
44:7-35	Old-age, permanent disability assistance.
52:4B-30	Crime victims' compensation.

INSURANCE

A:9-57.6	Civil defense workers' disability, death, medical or hospital benefits.
17:18-12; 17B:24-8	Health and disability benefits.
17:44A-19	Fraternal benefit society benefits.
17B:24-6	Life insurance proceeds, dividends, interest, loan, cash or surrender value, if you are not the insured.
17B:24-7	Annuity contract proceeds up to $500 per month.
17B:24-9	Group life or health policy or proceeds.
17B:24-10	Life insurance proceeds if policy prohibits use to pay creditors.
38A:4-8	Military member disability or death benefits.

MISCELLANEOUS

42:1A-27	Business partnership property.
Other	Add any applicable Federal Non-Bankruptcy Exemptions.

NOTE: *The symbol "§" or "§§" stands for section or sections of the statutes or code in your state. It refers to the particular part of the statutes of code listed here to the left of all references. A law librarian can help you.*

NEW MEXICO

New Mexico Statutes 1978 Annotated, Chapter 42, Section 42-10-9 (N.M.S.A. §42-10-9). Ignore volume numbers; look for "chapter" numbers. Compare Federal Bankruptcy Exemptions.

HOMESTEAD (**)
42-10-9	$30,000; includes "dwelling house" being purchased or leased (even if land on which it sits is owned by another).

PERSONAL PROPERTY
42-10-1	Motor vehicle up to $4,000; $500 of any property.
42-10-1; 42-10-2	Clothing; jewelry up to $2,500; books, furniture, and health equipment.
42-10-10	$2,000 of any property, in lieu of homestead.
48-2-15	Building materials.
53-4-28	Minimum amount of shares needed for membership in cooperative association.
70-4-12	Tools, machinery and materials needed to dig, drill, torpedo, complete, operate or repair an oil line, gas well or pipeline.

WAGES
35-12-7	Minimum of 75% of earned but unpaid wages. Judge may approve more for low income debtor.

PENSIONS
22-11-42	Public school employees.
42-10-1;	
42-10-2	Pension or retirement benefits.

PUBLIC BENEFITS
27-2-21	AFDC; general assistance.
31-22-15	Crime victims' compensation paid before July 1, 1993.
51-1-37	Unemployment compensation.
52-1-52	Workers' compensation.
52-3-37	Occupational disease disablement benefits.

TOOLS OF TRADE
42-10-1;	
42-10-2	$1,500.

INSURANCE
42-10-3	Life, accident, health or annuity benefits or cash value, if beneficiary is a citizen of New Mexico.
42-10-4	Benevolent association benefits up to $5,000.
42-10-5	Life insurance proceeds.
59A-44-18	Fraternal benefit society benefits.

MISCELLANEOUS
53-10-2	Ownership in an unincorporated association.
54-1A-501	Business partnership property.
Other	Add any applicable Federal Non-Bankruptcy Exemptions.

NEW YORK

References of numbers only are to *McKinney's* Consolidated Laws of New York, Civil Practice Law and Rules, Section 5206 (C.P.L.R. §5206). Other references are to "Debtor & Creditor" (D&C); "Estates, Powers & Trusts" (Est, Pow & Tr.); "Insurance" (Insur.); "Retirement & Social Security" (Ret. & Soc. Sec.); "Partnership" (Part.); and "Unconsolidated" (Unc.).

HOMESTEAD

5206   Real property, including mobile home, condominium or coop, up to $10,000.(**)

PERSONAL PROPERTY

5205   Clothing, furniture, refrigerator, TV, radio, sewing machine, security deposits with landlord or utility company, tableware, cooking utensils and crockery, stoves with food and fuel to last 60 days, health aids (including animals with food), church pew or seat, wedding ring, bible, school-books, pictures; books up to $50; burial plot without a structure to 1/4 acre; domestic animals with food to $450; watch to $35; trust fund principal; 90% of trust fund income.

D&C282   Motor vehicle up to $2,400; lost earnings recoveries needed for support; personal injury recoveries up to $7,500, not including pain and suffering; wrongful death recoveries for a person you depended upon for support.

D&C283   IN LIEU OF HOMESTEAD: Cash in the lesser amount of $2,500, or an amount when added to an annuity equals $5,000.

WAGES

5205   90% of earned but unpaid wages received within 60 days of filing for bankruptcy; 90% of earnings from milk sales to milk dealers; 100% for a few militia members.

PENSIONS

5205; D&C 282 ERISA-qualified plans, Keoghs and IRAs needed for support.
Insur. 4607   Public retirement benefits.
Ret. & Soc. Sec. 110   State employees.
Unc. 5711-o   Village police officers.

PUBLIC BENEFITS

D&C282   Unemployment benefits; veterans' benefits; social security; AFDC; aid to blind, aged and disabled; crime victims' compensation; home relief; local public assistance.

TOOLS OF TRADE

5205   Professional furniture, books, instruments, farm machinery, team and food for 60 days, up to $600 total; arms, swords, uniforms, equipment, horse, emblem and medal of a military member.

ALIMONY AND CHILD SUPPORT

D&C282   Alimony and child support needed for support.

INSURANCE

5205   Insurance proceeds for damaged exempt property.
5205; D&C283 Annuity contract benefits up to $5,000, if purchased within 6 months of filing for bankruptcy and not tax-deferred.
Est,Pow&Tr.7-1.5   Life insurance proceeds if policy prohibits use to pay creditors.
Insur.3212   Fraternal benefit society benefits; disability or illness benefits up to $400 per month; life insurance proceeds, dividends, interest, loan, cash or surrender value if beneficiary is not the insured.

MISCELLANEOUS

Part. 51   Business partnership property.
Other   Add any applicable Federal Non-Bankruptcy Exemptions.

NOTE: *The symbol "§" or "§§" stands for* section *or* sections *of the statutes or code in your state. It refers to the particular part of the statutes of code listed here to the left of all references. A law librarian can help you.*

NORTH CAROLINA

General Statutes of North Carolina, Chapter 1C, Section 1C-1601 (G.S.N.C. §1C-1601). Ignore volume numbers; look for "chapter" numbers.

HOMESTEAD

1C-1601   Real or personal property used as a residence, including coop, up to $10,000. Tenancies by the entirety exempt without limit as to debts of one spouse [*In re Crouch*, 33 B.R. 271 (E.D. N.C. 1983)].

PERSONAL PROPERTY

1C-1601   Motor vehicle up to $1,500; health aids; clothing, household goods, furnishings, appliances, books, animals, musical instruments and crops up to $3,500 total, plus additional $750 per dependent up to 4 dependents; personal injury and wrongful death recoveries for a person you depended upon; $3,500 of any property, less any amount claimed for homestead or burial plot.

1C-1601   Burial plot up to $10,000, in lieu of homestead.

1C-1601 $3,500 of any property, less any amount claimed for homestead or burial plot.

WAGES

1-362   Earned but unpaid wages received 60 days before filing for bankruptcy.

PENSIONS

58-86-90	Firefighters and rescue squad workers.
120-4.29	Legislators.
128-31	Municipal, city and county employees.
135-9;135-95	Teachers and state employees.
143-166.30	Law enforcement officers.

PUBLIC BENEFITS

15B-17	Crime victims' compensation.
96-17	Unemployment compensation.
97-21	Workers' compensation.
108A-36	AFDC; special adult assistance.
111-18	Aid to blind.

TOOLS OF TRADE

1C-1601   Tools, books and implements of trade up to $750.

INSURANCE

Const.10-5	Life insurance policy if beneficiary is insured spouse or child.
58-58-115	Life insurance proceeds, dividends, interest, loan, cash or surrender value.
58-58-165	Group life insurance policy or proceeds.
58-58-165	Employee group life policy or proceeds.
58-24-85	Fraternal benefit society benefits.

MISCELLANEOUS

59-55	Business partnership property.
Other	Add any applicable Federal Non-Bankruptcy Exemptions.

NORTH DAKOTA

North Dakota Century Code Annotated, Title 28, Chapter 28-22, Section 28-22-02 (N.D.C.C. §28-22-02). Ignore volume numbers; look for "title" numbers.

HOMESTEAD
28-22-02; 47-18-01   Real property, mobile home or house trailer up to $80,000.

PERSONAL PROPERTY
The following list applies to all debtors:
28-22-02   Clothing; fuel to last 1 year; bible; books up to $100; pictures; church pew; burial plots; crops or grain raised on the debtor's tract of land, limited to 1 tract of 160 acres.
28-22-03.1   Motor vehicle up to $1,200; personal injury recoveries not including pain and suffering, up to $7,500; wrongful death recoveries up to $7,500.
28-22-03.1   IN LIEU OF HOMESTEAD: cash to $7,500.

The following list applies to the head of household, not claiming crops or grain:
28-22-03 $5,000 of any personal property; OR
28-22-04   Furniture and bedding up to $1,000; books and musical instruments up to $1,500; tools and library of a professional up to $1,000; tools of a mechanic and stock in trade up to $1,000; and farm implements and livestock up to $4,500.

The following list applied to a non-head of household not claiming crops:
28-22-05 $2,500 of any personal property.

WAGES
32-09.1-.03   Minimum of 75% of earned but unpaid wages. Judge may approve more for low income debtor.

PENSIONS
28-22-03.1   Disabled veterans' benefits (does not include military retirement pay); annuities, pensions, IRAs, Keoghs, simplified employee plans (together with the insurance exemption under this section total may not exceed $200,000, although no limit if needed for support).
28-22-19   Public employees.

PUBLIC BENEFITS
28-22-03.1   Social security.
28-22-19   AFDC; crime victims' compensation.
37-25-07   Vietnam veterans' adjustment compensation.
52-06-30   Unemployment compensation.
65-05-29   Workers' compensation.

TOOLS OF TRADE
     See personal property section.

INSURANCE
26.1-15.1-18; 26.1-33-40   Fraternal benefit society benefits.
26.1-33-40   Life insurance proceeds payable to the decedent's estate.
28-22-03.1   Life insurance surrender value to $100,000 per policy if beneficiary is relative of the insured and policy was owned for more than 1 year before filing for bankruptcy. Together with pension exemption in this section, total cannot exceed $200,000, or $100,000 per plan, but no limit if needed for support.

MISCELLANEOUS
45-17-01   Business partnership property.
Other   Add any applicable Federal Non-Bankruptcy Exemptions.

NOTE: *The symbol "§" or "§§" stands for section or sections of the statutes or code in your state. It refers to the particular part of the statutes of code listed here to the left of all references. A law librarian can help you.*

OHIO

Page's Ohio Revised Code, Title 23, Section 2329.66 (O.R.C. §2329.66).

HOMESTEAD

2329.66   Real or personal property used as a residence up to $5,000. Tenancies by the entirety are exempt without limit as to debts of one spouse [*In re Thomas*, 14 B.R. 423 (N.D. Ohio 1981)].

PERSONAL PROPERTY

517.09;2329.66 Burial plot.

2329.66   (1) motor vehicle up to $1,000; (2) clothing, beds and bedding up to $200 per item; (3) cooking unit and refrigerator up to $300 each; (4) cash, bank and security deposits, tax refund and money due within 90 days up to $400 total (may include earnings not otherwise exempt); (5) household goods, furnishings, appliances, jewelry, books, animals, musical instruments, firearms, hunting and fishing equipment and crops up to $200 per item (see LIMIT below); (6) jewelry, up to $400 for one piece and up to $200 for each other piece (see LIMIT below); (7) health aids; (8) wrongful death recoveries for person you depended upon for support; (9) compensation for lost future earnings needed for support; (10) personal injury recoveries not including pain and suffering up to $5,000; and (11) $400 of any property. LIMIT: If homestead is not claimed, items under (5) and (6) may not exceed $2,000 total ($1,500 if homestead is claimed). **NOTE:** Section 2329.66 is relatively detailed and complex, so be sure to read it.

WAGES

2329.66   Minimum of 75% of earned but unpaid wages. Judge may approve more for low income debtor.

PENSIONS

145.56   Public employees.

146.13   Volunteer firefighters' dependents.

742.47   Police officers and firefighters.

2329.66   Police officers' and firefighters' death benefits; ERISA-qualified benefits, IRAs and Keoghs needed for support.

3307.71;3309.66 Public school employees.

5505.22   State highway patrol employees.

PUBLIC BENEFITS

2329.66;4123.67	Workers' compensation.	2329.66; 5115.07	Disability assistance.
2329.66;4141.32	Unemployment compensation.	2743.66	Crime victims' compensation.
2329.66;5107.12	AFDC.	3304.19	Vocational rehabilitation benefits.

TOOLS OF TRADE

147.04   Seal and official register of a notary public.

2329.66   Tools, books, and implements of trade up to $750.

ALIMONY AND CHILD SUPPORT

2329.66   Alimony and child support needed for support.

INSURANCE

2329.63;2329.66 Benevolent society benefits to $5,000.

2329.66;3917.05 Group life insurance policy or proceeds.

2329.66;3921.18 Fraternal benefit society benefits.

2329.66;3923.19 Disability benefits to $600 per month.

3911.10   Life, endowment or annuity contract dividends, interest, loan, cash or surrender value for your spouse, child or other dependent.

3911.12   Life insurance proceeds for spouse.

3911.14   Life insurance proceeds if policy prohibits use to pay creditors.

MISCELLANEOUS

1775.24; 2329.66 Business partnership property.

Other   Add any applicable Federal Non-Bankruptcy Exemptions.

OKLAHOMA

Oklahoma Statutes Annotated. Title 31, Section 2 (31 O.S.A. §2).

HOMESTEAD

31-2   Real property or manufactured home of unlimited value, but cannot exceed 160 acres if not in a city or town, or 1 acre in a city or town. Can be 160 acres if property was annexed by a city or town on or after 11/1/97. Can be more than one parcel. You do not need to occupy the home as long as you don't acquire another. May be limited to $5,000 if more than 25% of area of improvements is used for business purposes.

PERSONAL PROPERTY

8-7   Burial plots.

31-1   Motor vehicle up to $3,000; clothing up to $4,000; furniture, books, portraits, pictures, gun and health aids; food to last 1 year; 2 bridles and 2 saddles; 100 chickens, 20 sheep, 10 hogs, 5 cows and calves under 6 months, 2 horses and forage for livestock to last 1 year; personal injury, workers' compensation and wrongful death recoveries (not to include punitive damages) up to $50,000 total.

WAGES

12-1171.1;31-1   75% of wages earned within 90 days prior to filing bankruptcy. Judge may approve more if you can show hardship.

PENSIONS

11-49-126	Firefighters.	31-7	Disabled veterans.
11-50-124	Police officers.	47-2-303.3	Law enforcement employees.
19-959	County employees.	60-328	Tax exempt benefits.
31-1	ERISA-qualified benefits.	70-17-109	Teachers.

PUBLIC BENEFITS

21-142.13   Crime victims' compensation.

40-2-303   Unemployment compensation.

56-173   AFDC; social security.

85-48   Workers' compensation.

TOOLS OF TRADE

31-1   Tools, books, apparatus of trade, and husbandry implements to farm homestead, up to $5,000 total.

ALIMONY AND CHILD SUPPORT

31-1   Alimony and child support.

INSURANCE

36-2410   Assessment or mutual benefits.

36-2510   Limited stock insurance benefits.

36-2720   Fraternal benefit society benefits.

36-3631   Life insurance policy or proceeds if you are not the insured.

36-3632   Group life insurance policy or proceeds if you are not the insured.

36-6125   Funeral benefits if pre-paid and placed in trust.

MISCELLANEOUS

54-1-501   Business partnership property.

Other   Add any applicable Federal Non-Bankruptcy Exemptions.

OREGON

Oregon Revised Statutes Annotated, Chapter 23, Section 23.164 (O.R.S. §23.164). Ignore volume numbers; look for "chapter" numbers. All exemptions may be doubled by husband and wife [*In re Wilson*, 22 B.R. 146 (D. Ore. 1982)].

HOMESTEAD
23.164;23.250;
23.240   Real property, houseboat, or mobile home on land you own up to $25,000 ($33,000 if joint owners). Mobile home on land you don't own, $23,000 ($30,000 if joint). Property may not exceed 1 block in a city or town, or 160 acres elsewhere. Must occupy or intend to at time of filing. Sale proceeds exempt 1 year if plan to purchase another home.

PERSONAL PROPERTY
23.160   Motor vehicle to $1,700(**); clothing, jewelry, personal items to $1,800 total(**); household items, furniture, utensils, TVs and radios to $3,000 total; health aids; cash for sold exempt property; books, pictures & musical instruments to $600 total(**); food & fuel to last 60 days if debtor is householder; domestic animals & poultry with food to last 60 days to $1,000; lost earnings payments for debtor or someone debtor depended upon needed for support(**); personal injury recoveries (not pain and suffering) to $7,500(**); $400 of any personal property (can't be used to increase an existing exemption).
23.166   Bank deposits up to $7,500, and cash for sold exempt items.
23.200   Pistol; rifle or shotgun if owned by person over the age of 16, up to $1,000.
65.870   Burial plot.

WAGES
23.185   Minimum of 75% of earned but unpaid wages. Judge may approve more for low income debtor.
292.070   Wages withheld in a state employee's bond saving account.

PENSIONS
23.170   Federal, state or local government employees. ERISA-qualified benefits, if deposited at least 1 year before filing (IRAs, but not Keoghs).
237.201   Public officers and employees.
239.261   School district employees.

PUBLIC BENEFITS
23.160;147.325	Crime victims' compensation (**).	413.610	Old-age assistance.
344.580	Vocational rehabilitation.	414.095	Medical assistance.
401.405	Civil and disaster relief.	418.040	AFDC.
411.760	General assistance.	655.530	Injured inmates benefits.
412.115	Aid to blind.	656.234	Workers' compensation.
412.610	Aid to disabled.	657.855	Unemployment compensation.

TOOLS OF TRADE
23.160   Tools, implements, apparatus, team, harness, or library, up to $3,000 total (**).

ALIMONY AND CHILD SUPPORT
23.160   Alimony and child support needed to support.

INSURANCE
732.240   Life insurance proceeds if policy prohibits use to pay creditors.
743.046   Life insurance proceeds or cash value if you are not the insured.
743.047   Group life insurance policy or proceeds.
743.049   Annuity contract benefits up to $500 per month.
743.050   Health or disability insurance proceeds, dividends, interest, loan, cash or surrender value.
748.225   Fraternal benefit society benefits.

MISCELLANEOUS
68.420   Business partnership property.
471.301   Liquor licenses.
Other   Add any applicable Federal Non-Bankruptcy Exemptions.

NOTE: *The symbol "§" or "§§" stands for section or sections of the statutes or code in your state. It refers to the particular part of the statutes of code listed here to the left of all references. A law librarian can help you.*

PENNSYLVANIA

Purdon's Pennsylvania Statutes Annotated, Title 42, Section 8123 (42 Pa.C.S.A. §8123). Compare federal exemptions.

HOMESTEAD

None, but tenancies by the entirety are exempt without limit as to debts of one spouse [*In re McCormick*, 18 B.R. 911 (W.D. Pa. 1982)].

PERSONAL PROPERTY

42-8123	$300 of any property.
42-8124	Clothing, bibles, school books, sewing machines, uniform and accoutrements.
42-8125	Tangible personal property at an international exhibition sponsored by the U.S. government.

WAGES

42-8127	Earned but unpaid wages.

PENSIONS

16-4716	County employees.
24-8533; 42-8124	Public school employees.
42-8124	Private retirement benefits if plan provides benefits are not assignable; and self-employment retirement or annuity funds. Also plans under the following sections of the Internal Revenue Code: §401(a); annuity plans [§403(a)]; educational annuities [§403(b)]; IRAs [§408]; and employee stock ownership plans [§409]; up to $15,000 per year deposited and if deposited at least 1 year before filing.
53-764;53-776; 53-23666	Police officers.
42-8124; 53-881.115	Municipal employees.
53-13445; 53-23572; 53-39383	City employees.
42-8124; 71-5953	State employees.

PUBLIC BENEFITS

42-8124	Workers' compensation.
43-863	Unemployment compensation.
51-20012	Veterans' benefits.
51-20098	Korean conflict veterans' benefits.
71-180-7.10	Crime victims' compensation.

INSURANCE

42-8124	Fraternal benefit society benefits; insurance or annuity payments up to $100 per month; annuity or life insurance proceeds retained by insurer at maturity or otherwise if policy provides such proceeds are not assignable; group insurance policy or proceeds; annuity or life insurance proceeds if beneficiary is decedent's spouse, child, or other dependent relative; accident or disability insurance proceeds; no-fault automobile insurance proceeds.

MISCELLANEOUS

15-8342	Business partnership property.
Other	Add any applicable Federal Non-Bankruptcy Exemptions.

RHODE ISLAND

General Laws of Rhode Island, Section 7-8-25 (G.L.R.I. §7-8-25). Ignore "title" and "chapter" numbers; look for "section" numbers. Compare with federal exemptions.

PERSONAL PROPERTY

7-8-25	Consumer cooperative association holdings up to $50.
9-26-3	Body of a deceased person.
9-26-4	Clothing needed; furniture and family stores of a housekeeper, beds and bedding up to $1,000 total; books up to $300; burial plot; debt owed to you which is secured by a promissory note or bill of exchange.

WAGES

9-26-4	Earned but unpaid wages up to $50; wages of spouse; earned but unpaid wages of a seaman, or if you have received welfare during the year prior to filing for bankruptcy; wages paid to the poor by a charitable organization; earnings of a minor child.
30-7-9	Earned but unpaid wages of a military member on active duty.

PENSIONS

9-26-4	ERISA-qualified benefits.
9-26-5	Police officers and firefighters.
28-17-4	Private employees.
36-10-34	State and municipal employees.

PUBLIC BENEFITS

28-33-27	Workers' compensation.
28-41-32	State disability benefits.
28-44-58	Unemployment compensation.
30-7-9	Veterans' disability or survivor benefits.
40-6-14	AFDC; general assistance; aid to blind, aged and disabled.

TOOLS OF TRADE

9-26-4	Working tools up to $500; library of a professional in practice.

INSURANCE

27-4-11	Life insurance proceeds, dividends, interest, loan, cash or surrender value if beneficiary is not the insured.
27-4-12	Life insurance proceeds if policy prohibits use to pay creditors.
27-18-24	Accident or illness proceeds, benefits, dividends, interest, loan, cash or surrender value.
27-25-18	Fraternal benefit society benefits.
28-41-32	Temporary disability insurance.

MISCELLANEOUS

7-12-36	Business partnership property.
Other	Add any applicable Federal Non-Bankruptcy Exemptions.

NOTE: *The symbol "§" or "§§" stands for* section *or* sections *of the statutes or code in your state. It refers to the particular part of the statutes of code listed here to the left of all references. A law librarian can help you.*

SOUTH CAROLINA

Code of Laws of South Carolina, Title 15, Section 15-41-30 (C.L.S.C. §15-41-30). Ignore volume numbers; look for "title" numbers.

HOMESTEAD
15-41-30   Real property, personal property used as homestead (mobile home), or coop, up to $5,000. (**)

PERSONAL PROPERTY
15-41-30   Motor vehicle up to $1,200; clothing, household goods, furnishings, appliances, books, musical instruments, animals and crops up to $2,500 total; jewelry up to $500; health aids; personal injury and wrongful death recoveries.
15-41-30   IN LIEU OF HOMESTEAD: Burial plot up to $5,000.(**)
15-41-30   IN LIEU OF HOMESTEAD AND BURIAL PLOT: Cash and other liquid assets up to $1,000.

PENSIONS
9-1-1680   Public employees.
9-8-190   Judges and solicitors.
9-9-180   General assembly members.
9-11-270   Police officers.
9-13-230   Firefighters.
15-41-30   ERISA-qualified benefits.

PUBLIC BENEFITS
15-41-30   Unemployment compensation; social security; veterans' benefits.
15-41-30; 16-3-1300   Crime victims' compensation.
42-9-360   Workers' compensation.
43-5-190   AFDC; general relief; aid to blind, aged and disabled.

TOOLS OF TRADE
15-41-30   Tools, books and implements of trade up to $750 total.

ALIMONY AND CHILD SUPPORT
15-41-30   Alimony and child support.

INSURANCE
15-41-30   Unmatured life insurance contract (but a credit insurance policy is not exempt); disability or illness benefits; life insurance proceeds from a policy for a person you depended upon which is needed for support; life insurance dividends, interest, loan, cash or surrender value from a policy for a person you depended upon up to $4,000.
38-37-870   Fraternal benefit society benefits.
38-63-40   Life insurance proceeds for a spouse or child up to $25,000.
38-63-50   Life insurance proceeds if policy prohibits use to pay creditors.

MISCELLANEOUS
33-41-720   Business partnership property.
Other   Add any applicable Federal Non-Bankruptcy Exemptions.

NOTE: *The symbol "§" or "§§" stands for* section *or* sections *of the statutes or code in your state. It refers to the particular part of the statutes of code listed here to the left of all references. A law librarian can help you.*

SOUTH DAKOTA

South Dakota Codified Laws, Title 43, Chapter 31, Section 43-31-1 (S.D.C.L. §43-31-1). Ignore volume numbers; look for "title" numbers.

HOMESTEAD
43-31-1; 43-31-2   Real property, including mobile home if larger than 240 square feet and registered in the State at least 6 months prior to filing bankruptcy, of unlimited value; but cannot exceed 1 acre in a town or 160 acres elsewhere. Sale proceeds are exempt for 1 year after sale up to $30,000 (of unlimited value if you are an unmarried widow or widower, or are over 70). Spouse or child of a deceased owner may also claim exemption. Can't include gold or silver mine, mill or smelter. 43-31-5.

PERSONAL PROPERTY
43-45-2   All debtors may claim clothing; food and fuel to last 1 year; bible; books up to $200; pictures; church pew; burial plot; all property in South Dakota if judgment is in favor of any state for failure to pay that state's income tax on benefits received from a pension or other retirement plan while the judgment debtor was a resident of South Dakota.

43-45-4 $4,000 of any personal property; $6,000 if head of family.

WAGES
15-20-12   Earned wages owing 60 days prior to filing for bankruptcy, needed for support.

24-8-10   Wages of prisoners in work programs.

PENSIONS
3-12-115   Public employees.

9-16-47   City employees.

PUBLIC BENEFITS
28-7-16   AFDC.

61-6-28   Unemployment compensation.

62-4-42   Workers' compensation.

TOOLS OF TRADE
   See Personal Property.

INSURANCE
43-45-6   Life insurance proceeds if beneficiary is surviving spouse or child up to $10,000.

58-12-4   Health benefits up to $20,000; endowment or life insurance policy, proceeds or cash value up to $20,000(*).

58-12-8   Annuity contract proceeds up to $250 per month.

58-15-70   Life insurance proceeds if policy prohibits use to pay creditors.

58-37-68   Fraternal benefit society benefits.

MISCELLANEOUS
48-7A-501   Business partnership property.

Other   Add any applicable Federal Non-Bankruptcy Exemptions.

NOTE: *The symbol "§" or "§§" stands for* section *or* sections *of the statutes or code in your state. It refers to the particular part of the statutes of code listed here to the left of all references. A law librarian can help you.*

TENNESSEE

Tennessee Code Annotated, Title 26, Section 26-2-301 (T.C.A. §26-2-301). Ignore volume numbers; look for "section" numbers.

HOMESTEAD

26-2-301	$5,000; $7,500 for joint owners. Tenancies by the entirety are exempt without limit as to debts of one spouse [*In re Arango*, 136 B.R. 740; affirmed 992 F.2d 611 (6th Cir. 1993)]. Spouse or child of deceased owner may claim. May also claim a life estate or a 2 to 15 year lease.

PERSONAL PROPERTY

26-2-103	$4,000 of any personal property.
26-2-104	Clothing and storage containers; schools books, pictures, portraits, and bible.
26-2-111	Health aids; lost earnings payments for yourself or a person you depended upon; personal injury recoveries, not including pain and suffering, up to $7,500; wrongful death recoveries up to $10,000 (LIMIT: total of personal injury claims, wrongful death claims and crime victims' compensation cannot exceed $15,000).
26-2-305; 46-2-102	Burial plot up to 1 acre.

WAGES

26-2-106;	
26-2-107	Minimum of 75% of earned but unpaid wages, plus $2.50 per week per child. Judge may approve more for low income debtor.

PENSIONS

8-36-111	Public employees.
26-2-105	State and local government employees.
26-2-111	ERISA-qualified benefits.
45-9-909	Teachers.

PUBLIC BENEFITS

26-2-111	Unemployment compensation; veterans' benefits; social security; local public assistance, and Families First program benefits.
26-2-111;	
29-13-111	Crime victims' compensation up to $5,000, but see" LIMIT" under Personal Property above.
50-6-223	Workers' compensation.
71-2-216	Old-age assistance.
71-3-121	AFDC.
71-4-117	Aid to blind.
71-4-1112	Aid to disabled.

TOOLS OF TRADE

26-2-111	Tools, books and implements of trade up to $1,900.

ALIMONY AND CHILD SUPPORT

26-2-111	Alimony and child support which is owed for at least 30 days prior to filing for bankruptcy.

INSURANCE

26-2-110	Disability, accident or health benefits, for a resident and citizen of Tennessee.
26-2-111	Disability or illness benefits.
26-2-304	Homeowners' insurance proceeds up to $5,000.
56-7-201	Life insurance proceeds or cash value if beneficiary is the debtor's spouse, child or other dependent.
56-25-208	Fraternal benefit society benefits.

MISCELLANEOUS

61-1-124	Business partnership property.
Other	Add any applicable Federal Non-Bankruptcy Exemptions.

NOTE: *The symbol "§" or "§§" stands for section or sections of the statutes or code in your state. It refers to the particular part of the statutes of code listed here to the left of all references. A law librarian can help you.*

TEXAS

There are two sets of books that contain the Texas laws. One is called *Vernon's* Texas Civil Statutes, and is arranged by section number. The other is called *Vernon's* Texas Codes Annotated, and is divided into subjects, such as "Property," Insurance," "Human Resources," etc. The references given below that begin with just a number are references to the Civil Statutes (such as "110B-21.005"). The references that begin with a word are references to the subject volume or volumes of the Codes (such as "Prop. 41.001"). Compare Federal Bankruptcy Exemptions.

HOMESTEAD

Prop. 41.001; Prop. 41.002   Unlimited amount, but cannot exceed 1 acre in a city, town or village, or 100 acres (200 acres for family) elsewhere. Sale proceeds are exempt for 6 months after sale. You need not occupy at filing, as long as you don't acquire another home.

PERSONAL PROPERTY

Prop. 41.001   Burial plots.
Prop. 42.001   Prescribed health aids.
Prop. 42.002   Home furnishings, including family heirlooms; food; clothing; jewelry up to 25% of the SPECIAL LIMIT stated below; 2 firearms; athletic & sporting equipment (includes bicycles); 1 motor vehicle for each adult with drivers license or who relies on another to operate a vehicle; 2 horses, mules, or donkeys, with saddle, blanket & bridle for each; 12 head cattle; 60 head other livestock; 120 fowl; food on hand for these animals; and household pets. **SPECIAL LIMIT:** Total of all items under Property 42.002 (including tools of trade and cash value of life insurance) cannot exceed $30,000 total ($60,000 for head of family).

WAGES

Prop. 42.001   Current wages for personal services; and unpaid commissions for personal services up to 25% of the SPECIAL LIMIT stated above.

PENSIONS

110B-21.005	State employees.	6243d-1;6243j; 6243g-1	Police officers.
110B-31.005	Teachers.	6243e;6243e.1; 6243e.2	Firefighters.
110B-41.004	Judges.	6243g; 110B-61.006	Municipal employees.
110B-51.006	County and district employees.	Prop. 42.0021	Church benefits; ERISA-qualified retirement benefits to extent tax-deferred, including IRAs, Keoghs & simplified employee plans.
6228f	Law enforcement officers' survivors.		

PUBLIC BENEFITS

5221b-13	Unemployment compensation.	Hum.Res. 31.040	AFDC.
8306-3	Workers' compensation.	Hum.Res. 32.036	Medical assistance.
8309-1	Crime victims' compensation.		

TOOLS OF TRADE

Prop. 42.002   Tools, books, and equipment, including motor vehicles and boats used in trade or profession; and farming or ranching vehicles and implements.

INSURANCE

Insur. 3.50-2   Texas employee uniform group insurance.
Insur. 3.50-3   Texas state college or university employee benefits.
Insur. 3.50-4   Retired public school employees group insurance.
Insur. 10.28   Fraternal benefit society benefits.
Insur. 21.22   Life, health, accident or annuity benefits; life insurance proceeds if policy prohibits use to pay creditors.
Prop. 42.002   Life insurance cash value if beneficiary is debtor or family member.

MISCELLANEOUS

6132b-2.04   Business partnership property.
Other   Add any applicable Federal Non-Bankruptcy Exemptions.

UTAH

Utah Code Annotated 1953, Title 78, Chapter 23, Section 78-23-3 (U.C.A. §78-23-3). Ignore volume numbers; look for "title" numbers.

HOMESTEAD(**)

78-23-3   Real property or mobile home (land may not exceed 1 acre), up to $5,000 if some or all of property is not debtor's primary personal residence; up to $20,000 if all of property is debtor's primary personal residence. May be claimed on more than one parcel. Proceeds of sale exempt for 1 year. Water rights and interests, in the form of corporate stock or otherwise, are exempt to extent they are necessarily employed in supplying water to the homestead for domestic and irrigating purposes.

PERSONAL PROPERTY

78-23-5   Clothing, except furs and jewelry; refrigerator, freezer, stove, microwave oven, washer, dryer, and sewing machine; health aids; food to last 12 months; beds and bedding; carpets; artwork done by, or depicting, a family member, if not part of trade or business; burial plot; personal injury recoveries for yourself or a person you depend upon; wrongful death recoveries for a person you depended upon.

78-23-8   Sofas, chairs, and related furnishings for one household up to $500; dining and kitchen tables and chairs for one household up to $500; animals, books, and musical instruments up to $500; heirlooms or other items of sentimental value up to $500.

78-23-9   Proceeds for damaged personal property.

WAGES

70C-7-103   Minimum of 75% of earned but unpaid wages. Judge may approve more for low income debtor.

PENSIONS

49-1-609   Public employees.
78-23-5   ERISA-qualified benefits.
78-23-6   Any pension needed for support.

PUBLIC BENEFITS

35-1-80   Workers' compensation.
35-2-35   Occupational disease disability benefits.
35-4-18   Unemployment compensation.
55-15-32   AFDC; general assistance.
63-63-21   Crime victims' compensation.
78-23-5   Veterans' benefits.

TOOLS OF TRADE

39-1-47   Military property of a national guard member.
78-23-8   Motor vehicle used in business or trade up to $2,500 (does not qualify if only used for transportation to and from work); tools, books, and implements of trade up to $3,500.

ALIMONY AND CHILD SUPPORT

78-23-5   Child support.
78-23-6   Alimony needed for support.

INSURANCE

31A-9-603   Fraternal benefit society benefits.
78-23-5   Disability, illness, medical or hospital benefits.
78-23-6   Life insurance proceeds if beneficiary is insured's spouse or other dependent, needed for support.
78-23-7   Life insurance policy cash surrender value up to $5,000.

MISCELLANEOUS

48-1-22   Business partnership property.
Other   Add any applicable Federal Non-Bankruptcy Exemptions.

VERMONT

Vermont Statutes Annotated, Title 27, Section 101 (27 V.S.A. §101). Look for "title" numbers. Compare Federal Bankruptcy Exemptions.

HOMESTEAD
27-101 $75,000. May include outbuildings, rents, issues, and profits. Spouse of deceased owner may claim (27 V.S.A. §105). Tenancies by the entirety are exempt without limit as to debts of one spouse [In re McQueen, 21 B.R. 736 (D. Ver. 1982)].

PERSONAL PROPERTY
12-2740   Motor vehicles up to $2,500; clothing, goods, furnishings, appliances, books, musical instruments, animals and crops up to $2,500 total; refrigerator, stove, freezer, water heater, heating unit and sewing machines; health aids; bank deposits up to $700; wedding ring; jewelry up to $500; 500 gallons of oil, 5 tons of coal or 10 cords of firewood; 500 gallons of bottled gas; lost future earnings for yourself or a person you depended upon; personal injury and wrongful death recoveries for a person you depended upon; 1 cow, 10 sheep, 10 chickens, 3 swarms of bees, and feed to last 1 winter; 1 yoke of oxen or steers, 2 horses, 2 harnesses, 2 halters, 2 chains, 1 plow and 1 ox yoke; growing crops up to $5,000.
12-2740 $400 of any property; plus $7,000, less any amount claimed for clothing, goods, furnishings, appliances, books, musical instruments, animals, crops, motor vehicle, jewelry, tools of trade and growing crops, of any property.

WAGES
12-3170   Minimum of 75% of earned but unpaid wages (judge may approve more for low income debtor); all wages if you received welfare during the 2 months prior to filing for bankruptcy.

PENSIONS
3-476   State employees.
12-2740   Self-directed accounts, including IRAs and Keoghs, up to $10,000; other pensions.
16-1946   Teachers.
24-5066   Municipal employees.

PUBLIC BENEFITS
12-2740   Veterans' benefits, social security and crime victims' compensation needed for support.
21-681   Workers' compensation.
21-1376   Unemployment compensation.
33-2575   AFDC; general assistance; aid to blind, aged and disabled.

TOOLS OF TRADE
12-2740   Tools and books of trade up to $5,000.

ALIMONY AND CHILD SUPPORT
12-2740   Alimony and child support needed for support.

INSURANCE
8-3705   Life insurance proceeds if policy prohibits use to pay creditors.
8-3706   Life insurance proceeds if insured is not the beneficiary.
8-3708   Group life or health benefits.
8-3709   Annuity contract benefits up to $350 per month.
8-4086   Health benefits up to $200 per month.
8-4478   Fraternal benefit society benefits.
12-2740   Unmatured life insurance contract (but not credit insurance policy); disability or illness benefits needed for support; life insurance proceeds for a person you depended upon.

MISCELLANEOUS
11-3241   Business partnership property.
Other   Add any applicable Federal Non-Bankruptcy Exemptions.

NOTE: *The symbol "§" or "§§" stands for* section *or* sections *of the statutes or code in your state. It refers to the particular part of the statutes of code listed here to the left of all references. A law librarian can help you.*

VIRGINIA

Code of Virginia 1950, Title 34, Section 34-4 (C.V. §34-4). Ignore "chapter" numbers; look for "title" and "section" numbers.

HOMESTEAD (**)

34-4	$5,000 [$7,000 for veterans with a 40% V.A.-rated service connected disability (34-4.1)], plus $500 per dependent. Tenancies by the entirety are exempt without limitation as to debts of one spouse [*In re Harris*, 155 B.R. 948 (E.D.Va. 1993)]. Includes rents and profits (34-18). Sale proceeds are exempt (34-20). Must file homestead declaration prior to filing for bankruptcy (34-6).

PERSONAL PROPERTY

34-4.1	$2,000 of any property of a disabled veteran who is a householder.
34-13	Unused homestead.
34-26	ONLY IF YOU ARE A HOUSEHOLDER YOU MAY CLAIM: Motor vehicle up to $2,000; wearing apparel up to $1,000; household furnishings up to $5,000; family portraits and heirlooms up to $5,000; burial plot; wedding and engagement rings, family Bible; animals owned as pets, provided they are not raised for sale or profit; and medically prescribed health aids.
34-13	IN LIEU OF HOMESTEAD: $5,000 of any personal property.

WAGES

34-29	Minimum of 75% of earned but unpaid wages or pension payments. Judge may approve more for low income debtor.

PENSIONS

51-111.15	State employees.
51-127.7	County employees.
51-180	Judges.

PUBLIC BENEFITS

19.2-368.12	Crime victims' compensation, unless seeking to discharge debt for treatment of crime-related injury.
60.2-600	Unemployment compensation.
63.1-88	AFDC; general relief; aid to blind, aged and disabled.
65.1-82	Workers' compensation.

TOOLS OF TRADE

ANYONE MAY CLAIM:

44-96	Arms, uniforms and equipment of a military member.

IF YOU ARE A HOUSEHOLDER YOU MAY ALSO CLAIM:

34-26	Tools, books, instruments, implements, equipment, and machines, including motor vehicles, vessels, and aircraft, necessary for use in occupation or trade up to $10,000.
34-27	For farmer: tractor, wagon, cart, horses, pair of mules with gear up to $3,000; fertilizer, 2 plows, harvest cradle, 2 iron wedges, pitchfork and rake, up to $1,000.

INSURANCE

38.2-3122	Life insurance proceeds, dividends, interest, loan, cash or surrender value if beneficiary is not the insured.
38.2-3123	If you are a householder, life insurance cash values up to $10,000.
38.2-3339	Group life insurance policy or proceeds.
38.2-3549	Accident, sickness or industrial sick benefits.
38.2-3811	Cooperative life insurance benefits.
38.2-4021	Burial society benefits.
38.2-4118	Fraternal benefit society benefits.
51-111.67:8	Group life or accident insurance for government officials.

MISCELLANEOUS

50-73.105	Business partnership property.
Other	Add any applicable Federal Non-Bankruptcy Exemptions.

WASHINGTON

West's Revised Code of Washington Annotated, Title 6, Chapter 6.13, Section 6.13.010 (R.C.W.A. §6.13.010). Compare Federal Bankruptcy Exemptions.

HOMESTEAD (*)

6.13.010	Real property or mobile home up to $40,000 [no limit on exemption if you are seeking to discharge a debt based on another state's claim of failure to pay that state income tax on pension or retirement benefits you received while a resident of Washington (6.13.030)]. If property is unimproved or unoccupied at time of filing bankruptcy, you must file a homestead declaration.

PERSONAL PROPERTY

6.15.010	2 motor vehicles up to $2,500 total; clothing, but furs, jewelry & ornaments limited to $1,000 total; household goods, furniture, appliances, food, fuel, home and yard equipment up to $2,700 total; books up to $1,000; pictures and keepsakes; private libraries up to $1,500; $1,000 of any other personal property, but not more than $100 of it in cash, bank deposits, stocks, bonds or other securities.
68.20.120	Burial plots if sold by a non-profit cemetery association.

WAGES

6.27.150	Minimum of 75% of earned but unpaid wages. Judge may approve more for low income debtor.

PENSIONS

6.15.020	Federal employees; ERISA-qualified benefits, including IRAs.
41.24.240	Volunteer firefighters.
41.28.200	City employees.
41.40.380	Public employees.
43.43.310	State patrol officers.

PUBLIC BENEFITS

7.68.070;	
51.32.040	Crime victims' compensation.
50.40.020	Unemployment compensation.
51.32.040	Industrial insurance (workers' compensation).
74.04.280	General assistance.
74.08.210	Old-age assistance.
74.13.070	AFDC.

TOOLS OF TRADE

6.15.010	Tools and materials used in another person's trade up to $5,000; library, office furniture, equipment and supplies of a physician, surgeon, attorney, clergyman or other professional up to $5,000; farm trucks, tools, equipment, supplies, stock and seed of a farmer up to $5,000.

INSURANCE

6.15.030	Insurance proceeds for destroyed exempt property.
46.18.400	Disability benefits, proceeds, dividends, interest, loan, cash or surrender value.
46.18.410	Life insurance proceeds, dividends, interest, loan, cash or surrender value if the insured is not the beneficiary.
46.18.420	Group life insurance policy or proceeds.
46.18.430	Annuity contract proceeds up to $250 per month.
48.36A.180	Fraternal benefit society benefits.

MISCELLANEOUS

25.05.200	Business partnership property.
Other	Add any applicable Federal Non-Bankruptcy Exemptions.

WEST VIRGINIA

West Virginia Code, Chapter 38, Article 10, Section 38-10-4 (.W.V.C. §38-10-4). Ignore volume numbers; look for "chapter" numbers.

HOMESTEAD
38-10-4   Real or personal property used as a residence up to $15,000. Unused portion may be applied to any other property.

PERSONAL PROPERTY
38-10-4   Motor vehicle up to $2,400; clothing, household goods, furnishings, appliances, books, musical instruments, animals and crops up to $400 per item, and $8,000 total; jewelry up to $1,000; health aids; lost earnings payments needed for support; personal injury recoveries, not including pain and suffering, up to $7,500; wrongful death recoveries for a person you depended upon needed for support; $800 of any property.

38-10-4 $7,900, less amount of homestead claimed, of any property.

38-10-4   Burial plot up to $15,000, in lieu of homestead.

WAGES
38-5A-3   80% of earned but unpaid wages. Judge may approve more for low income debtor.

PENSIONS
5-10-46   Public employees.
18-7A-30   Teachers.
38-10-4   ERISA-qualified benefits needed for support.

PUBLIC BENEFITS
9-5-1   AFDC; general assistance; aid to blind, aged and disabled.
14-2A-24; 38-10-4   Crime victims' compensation.
23-4-18   Workers' compensation.
38-10-4   Unemployment compensation; veterans' benefits; social security.

TOOLS OF TRADE
38-4-10   Tools, books and implements of trade up to $1,500.

ALIMONY AND CHILD SUPPORT
38-10-4   Alimony and child support needed for support.

INSURANCE
33-6-27   Life insurance proceeds unless you are policy owner and beneficiary.
33-6-28   Group life insurance policy and proceeds.
33-23-21   Fraternal benefit society benefits.
38-10-4   Unmatured life insurance contract (except for credit life insurance contract); health or disability benefits; life insurance dividends, interest, loan, cash or surrender value for person you depended upon up to $4,000.
48-3-23   Life insurance proceeds or cash value if the beneficiary is a married woman.

MISCELLANEOUS
47B-5-1   Business partnership property.
Other   Add any applicable Federal Non-Bankruptcy Exemptions.

NOTE: *The symbol "§" or "§§" stands for section or sections of the statutes or code in your state. It refers to the particular part of the statutes of code listed here to the left of all references. A law librarian can help you.*

WISCONSIN

West's Wisconsin Statutes Annotated, Section 815.20 (W.S.A. §815.20). Look for "section" numbers. Compare Federal Bankruptcy Exemptions.

HOMESTEAD
815.20 $40,000. Sale proceed exempt for 2 years after sale provided you intend to acquire another home. Must occupy or intend to occupy at time of filing for bankruptcy.

PERSONAL PROPERTY
815.18   Automobile up to $1,200 (plus any of the $5,000 household furnishings exemption that is unused); household goods and furnishings; wearing apparel, keepsakes, jewelry and other articles of adornment, appliances, books, musical instruments, firearms, sporting goods, animals or other items for family use up to $5,000 total; burial plot, monument, tombstone, etc.; and bank deposits up to $1,000; wrongful death proceeds and lost earnings compensation for debtor or person on whom debtor was dependent, to extent necessary to support debtor or family; and personal injury payments for debtor or person upon whom debtor depended, up to $25,000.

WAGES
815.18   75% of net wages, but limited to amount necessary for support, and no less that 30 times the state or federal minimum wage, whichever is greater.

PENSIONS
40.08   Public employees.
66.81   Certain municipal employees in a city of more 150,000 or more in population.
815.18   Police officers, firefighters, military pensions, and public and private retirement benefits (including plans for self-employed persons).

PUBLIC BENEFITS
45.35   Veterans' benefits.   108.13   Unemployment compensation.
49.41   AFDC; other social service payments.   949.07   Crime victims' compensation.
102.27   Workers' compensation.

TOOLS OF TRADE
815.18   Equipment, inventory, farm products, and professional books used in the business of the debtor or a dependent, up to $7,500.

ALIMONY AND CHILD SUPPORT
815.18   Alimony & child support needed for support.

INSURANCE
614.96   Fraternal benefit society benefits.
632.42   Life insurance proceeds if policy prohibits use to pay creditors.
815.18   Unmatured life insurance contracts, and up to $4,000 in value in accrued dividends, interest or loan value (except for credit life contracts) if owned by debtor and insuring debtor, dependent, or person debtor is dependent upon; federal disability benefits; life insurance proceeds if debtor was dependent upon insured, to extent necessary to support debtor or family; and fire insurance proceeds received during prior 2 years for destroyed exempt property.

MISCELLANEOUS
178.21   Business partnership property.
Other   Add any applicable Federal Non-Bankruptcy Exemptions.

WYOMING

Wyoming Statutes Annotated, Title 1, Chapter 20, Section 1-20-101 (W.S.A. §1-20-101). Ignore volume numbers; look for "title" numbers.

HOMESTEAD (**)

1-20-101; 1-20-104	Real property up to $10,000; house trailer up to $6,000. Tenancies by the entirety are exempt without limit as to debts of one spouse [*In re Anselmi*, 52 B.R. 479 (D. Wyo. 1985)]. Spouse or child of deceased owner may claim; Must occupy at time of filing for bankruptcy.

PERSONAL PROPERTY

1-20-105	Clothing and wedding rings up to $1,000 total.
1-20-106	Household articles, furniture, bedding and food up to $2,000 per person in the home; school books, pictures and bible; motor vehicle up to $2,400.
1-20-106; 35-8-104	Burial plot.
26-32-102	Pre-paid funeral contracts.

WAGES

1-15-511	Minimum of 75% of earned but unpaid wages. Judge may approved more for low income debtor.
17-16-308	Wages of inmates on work release.
19-2-501	Earnings of national guard members.

PENSIONS

1-20-110	Private or public retirement funds or accounts.
9-3-426	Public employees.
9-3-620	Highway officers, criminal investigators, and game and fish wardens.
15-5-209	Payments being received by police officers and firefighters.

PUBLIC BENEFITS

1-40-113	Crime victims' compensation.	27-14-702	Workers' compensation.
27-3-319	Unemployment compensation.	42-2-113	AFDC; general assistance.

TOOLS OF TRADE

1-20-106	Motor vehicle, tools, implements, team and stock in trade to $2,000; library and implements of a professional up to $2,000.

INSURANCE

1-20-111	Funds in a qualified medical savings account.
26-15-129	Life insurance proceeds if insured is not the beneficiary.
26-15-130	Disability benefits if policy prohibits use to pay creditors.
26-15-131	Group life or disability policy or proceeds.
26-15-132	Annuity contract proceeds up to $350 per month.
26-15-133	Life insurance proceeds if policy prohibits use to pay creditors.
26-29-116	Fraternal benefit society benefits.

MISCELLANEOUS

12-4-604	Liquor licenses and malt beverage permits.
17-21-501	Business partnership property.
Other	Add any applicable Federal Non-Bankruptcy Exemptions.

Appendix B
Checklists

This appendix has checklists for both a Chapter 7 and Chapter 13 filing. These include all items required for filing each type of bankruptcy. Use these checklists to ensure that you bring with you at all times the appropriate forms and materials.

TABLE OF CHECKLISTS

IF YOU ARE FILING FOR CHAPTER 7 BANKRUPTCY, YOU SHOULD BRING:

❏ VOLUNTARY PETITION (form __)

❏ SUMMARY OF SCHEDULES (form __)

❏ SCHEDULE A through SCHEDULE J (forms __ through __)

❏ DECLARATION CONCERNING DEBTOR'S SCHEDULES (form __)

❏ STATEMENT OF FINANCIAL AFFAIRS (form __)

❏ CHAPTER 7 INDIVIDUAL DEBTOR'S STATEMENT OF INTENTION (form __)

❏ Master Address List [either using the MAILING MATRIX (form 18) or other format as required by the court in which you will file your case]

❏ Check or money order for the filing fee.

❏ Note pad or paper, and pen, for writing down any information or instructions the court clerk may give you.

NOTE: *You may also be filing an* APPLICATION TO PAY FILING FEE IN INSTALLMENTS *(form __), which needs to be filed with your other documents. If you are filing this document, your check or money order should be for the amount of the first payment listed on form __. For either type of bankruptcy, be sure you have at least the number of copies required by the clerk, plus a copy for yourself.*

INCOME AND EXPENSE WORKSHEET

INCOME (Monthly):
    Take Home Pay (wages, salary, commissions)   _____
    Self Employment Income   _____
    Interest and Dividends   _____
    Income From Real Estate   _____
    Retirement Income   _____
    Alimony or Support Payments   _____
    Other:_____   _____

TOTAL MONTHLY INCOME   _____

EXPENSES (Monthly):
    Mortgage or Rent   _____
    Homeowners/Renters Insurance   _____
    Real Estate Taxes   _____
    Electricity   _____
    Gas   _____
    Water   _____
    Telephone   _____
    Garbage Pick-up   _____
    Other:_____   _____
    Home Repair/Maintenance   _____
    Auto Loan   _____
    Other Installment Loan Payments:

    _____   _____
    _____   _____
    _____   _____
    _____   _____

    Auto Insurance   _____
    Gasoline   _____
    Auto Repairs/Maintenance   _____
    Food   _____
    Clothing   _____
    Medical, Dental, and Medicines   _____
    Life Insurance   _____
    Laundry   _____
    Recreation/Travel/Entertainment   _____
    Education   _____
    License Fees, Dues, Memberships   _____
    Other Taxes   _____
    Other:_____   _____

    _____   _____
    _____   _____
    _____   _____
    _____   _____

TOTAL MONTHLY EXPENSES   _____

DEFICIT (Total Income - Total Expenses)   _____

PROPERTY WORKSHEET

(1) PROPERTY	(2) VALUE	(3) AMT. OWED	(4) EQUITY	(5) EXEMPT	(6) SECURED
Real Estate:					
Autos, etc.:					
Boats, etc.:					
Cash on hand:					
Bank accts:					
Clothing:					
Jewelry:					
Household Goods:					
Collections:					
Sports Equip:					
Trade tools:					
Investments:					
Insurance:					
Other prop:					
TOTALS:					

DEBT WORKSHEET

	(1) LENDER	(2) ITEM	(3) BALANCE	(4) SECURED	(5) DISCHARGEABLE
Real Estate:					
Autos, etc.:					
Boats, etc.:					
Credit Cards:					
Student Loans:					
Taxes Owed:					
Other Debts:					
TOTALS:					
	(1) LENDER	(2) ITEM	(3) BALANCE	(4) SECURED	(5) DISCHARGEABLE

MONTHLY BUDGET

TOTAL MONTHLY INCOME $\qquad$ \$_____

EXPENSES (Monthly):

Mortgage or Rent $\qquad$ \$_____
Homeowners/Renters Insurance \$_____
Real Estate Taxes \$_____
Electricity \$_____
Gas \$_____
Water \$_____
Telephone \$_____
Garbage Pick-up \$_____
Other:_____ \$_____
Home Repair/Maintenance \$_____
Auto Loan \$_____
Other Installment Loan Payments:

_____ \$_____
_____ \$_____
_____ \$_____
_____ \$_____
_____ \$_____

Auto Insurance \$_____
Gasoline \$_____
Auto Repairs/Maintenance \$_____
Food \$_____
Clothing \$_____
Medical, Dental, and Medicines \$_____
Life Insurance \$_____
Laundry \$_____
Recreation/Travel/Entertainment \$_____
Education \$_____
License Fees, Dues, Memberships \$_____
Other Taxes \$_____
Other:_____ \$_____
_____ \$_____
_____ \$_____
_____ \$_____
_____ \$_____

TOTAL MONTHLY EXPENSES \$_____

APPENDIX D
FORMS

This appendix contains the forms referred to in the various sections of this book. To use them, you should first tear them out and make photocopies of the ones you will need. Remember to punch the holes out at the top for easy filing by the clerk.

An asterisk (*) following the title of a form indicates that the form also has a continuation sheet to be used for additional information. The continuation sheet will be found immediately after the form in this appendix.

In 1991, bankruptcy forms were standardized throughout the country. However, you may find that your particular bankruptcy court has certain other required forms. Before you begin to prepare your forms, you should call the court clerk's office and ask if there are any special required forms. The current bankruptcy rules require the courts to accept the forms used in this book.

TABLE OF FORMS

United States Bankruptcy Court District of_____	Voluntary Petition

Name of Debtor (if individual, enter Last, First, Middle):	Name of Joint Debtor (Spouse) (Last, First, Middle):
All Other Names used by the Debtor in the last 6 years (include married, maiden, and trade names):	All Other Names used by the Joint Debtor in the last 6 years (include married, maiden, and trade names):
Soc. Sec./Tax I.D. No. (if more than one, state all):	Soc. Sec./Tax I.D. No. (if more than one, state all):
Street Address of Debtor (No. & Street, City, State & Zip Code):	Street Address of Joint Debtor (No. & Street, City, State & Zip Code):
County of Residence or of the Principal Place of Business:	County of Residence or of the Principal Place of Business:
Mailing Address of Debtor (if different from street address):	Mailing Address of Joint Debtor (if different from street address):

Location of Principal Assets of Business Debtor
(if different from street address above):

Information Regarding the Debtor (Check the Applicable Boxes)

Venue (Check any applicable box)
- ☐ Debtor has been domiciled or has had a residence, principal place of business, or principal assets in this District for 180 days immediately preceding the date of this petition or for a longer part of such 180 days than in any other District.
- ☐ There is a bankruptcy case concerning debtor's affiliate, general partner, or partnership pending in this District.

Type of Debtor (Check all boxes that apply)
- ☐ Individual(s)
- ☐ Corporation
- ☐ Partnership
- ☐ Other_____
- ☐ Railroad
- ☐ Stockbroker
- ☐ Commodity Broker
- ☐ Clearing Bank

Chapter or Section of Bankruptcy Code Under Which the Petition is Filed (Check one box)
- ☐ Chapter 7
- ☐ Chapter 9
- ☐ Chapter 11
- ☐ Chapter 12
- ☐ Chapter 13
- ☐ Sec. 304 - Case ancillary to foreign proceeding

Nature of Debts (Check one box)
- ☐ Consumer/Non-Business
- ☐ Business

Chapter 11 Small Business (Check all boxes that apply)
- ☐ Debtor is a small business as defined in 11 U.S.C. § 101
- ☐ Debtor is and elects to be considered a small business under 11 U.S.C. § 1121(e) (Optional)

Filing Fee (Check one box)
- ☐ Full Filing Fee attached
- ☐ Filing Fee to be paid in installments (Applicable to individuals only) Must attach signed application for the court's consideration certifying that the debtor is unable to pay fee except in installments. Rule 1006(b). See Official Form No. 3.

Statistical/Administrative Information (Estimates only)
- ☐ Debtor estimates that funds will be available for distribution to unsecured creditors.
- ☐ Debtor estimates that, after any exempt property is excluded and administrative expenses paid, there will be no funds available for distribution to unsecured creditors.

THIS SPACE IS FOR COURT USE ONLY

Estimated Number of Creditors	1-15	16-49	50-99	100-199	200-999	1000-over
	☐	☐	☐	☐	☐	☐

Estimated Assets	$0 to $50,000	$50,001 to $100,000	$100,001 to $500,000	$500,001 to $1 million	$1,000,001 to $10 million	$10,000,001 to $50 million	$50,000,001 to $100 million	More than $100 million
	☐	☐	☐	☐	☐	☐	☐	☐

Estimated Debts	$0 to $50,000	$50,001 to $100,000	$100,001 to $500,000	$500,001 to $1 million	$1,000,001 to $10 million	$10,000,001 to $50 million	$50,000,001 to $100 million	More than $100 million
	☐	☐	☐	☐	☐	☐	☐	☐

Voluntary Petition
(This page must be completed and filed in every case)

Name of Debtor(s):

Prior Bankruptcy Case Filed Within Last 6 Years (If more than one, attach additional sheet)

Location Where Filed:	Case Number:	Date Filed:

Pending Bankruptcy Case Filed by any Spouse, Partner or Affiliate of this Debtor (If more than one, attach additional sheet)

Name of Debtor:	Case Number:	Date Filed:
District:	Relationship:	Judge:

Signatures

Signature(s) of Debtor(s) (Individual/Joint)

I declare under penalty of perjury that the information provided in this petition is true and correct.

[If petitioner is an individual whose debts are primarily consumer debts and has chosen to file under chapter 7] I am aware that I may proceed under chapter 7, 11, 12 or 13 of title 11, United States Code, understand the relief available under each such chapter, and choose to proceed under chapter 7.

I request relief in accordance with the chapter of title 11, United States Code, specified in this petition.

X _____
Signature of Debtor

X _____
Signature of Joint Debtor

_____
Telephone Number (If not represented by attorney)

_____
Date

Signature of Attorney

X _____
Signature of Attorney for Debtor(s)

_____
Printed Name of Attorney for Debtor(s)

_____
Firm Name

_____
Address

_____
Telephone Number

_____
Date

Signature of Debtor (Corporation/Partnership)

I declare under penalty of perjury that the information provided in this petition is true and correct, and that I have been authorized to file this petition on behalf of the debtor.

The debtor requests relief in accordance with the chapter of title 11, United States Code, specified in this petition.

X _____
Signature of Authorized Individual

_____
Printed Name of Authorized Individual

_____
Title of Authorized Individual

_____
Date

Exhibit A

(To be completed if debtor is required to file periodic reports (e.g., forms 10K and 10Q) with the Securities and Exchange Commission pursuant to Section 13 or 15(d) of the Securities Exchange Act of 1934 and is requesting relief under chapter 11)

☐ Exhibit A is attached and made a part of this petition.

Exhibit B

(To be completed if debtor is an individual whose debts are primarily consumer debts)

I, the attorney for the petitioner named in the foregoing petition, declare that I have informed the petitioner that [he or she] may proceed under chapter 7, 11, 12, or 13 of title 11, United States Code, and have explained the relief available under each such chapter.

X _____
Signature of Attorney for Debtor(s)   Date

Exhibit C

Does the debtor own or have possession of any property that poses a threat of imminent and identifiable harm to public health or safety?

☐ Yes, and Exhibit C is attached and made a part of this petition.
☐ No

Signature of Non-Attorney Petition Preparer

I certify that I am a bankruptcy petition preparer as defined in 11U.S.C. § 110, that I prepared this document for compensation, and that I have provided the debtor with a copy of this document.

_____
Printed Name of Bankruptcy Petition Preparer

_____
Social Security Number

_____
Address

Names and Social Security numbers of all other individuals who prepared or assisted in preparing this document:

If more than one person prepared this document, attach additional sheets conforming to the appropriate official form for each person.

X _____
Signature of Bankruptcy Petition Preparer

_____
Date

A bankruptcy petition preparer's failure to comply with the provisions of title 11 and the Federal Rules of Bankruptcy Procedure may result in fines or imprisonment or both 11 U.S.C. §110; 18 U.S.C. §156.

UNITED STATES BANKRUPTCY COURT
DISTRICT OF _____

In re _____,
        Debtor

Case No. _____

Chapter _____

APPLICATION TO PAY FILING FEE IN INSTALLMENTS

1.   In accordance with Fed. R. Bankr. P. 1006, I apply for permission to pay the Filing Fee amounting to $_____ in installments.

2.   I certify that I am unable to pay the Filing Fee except in installments.

3.   I further certify that I have not paid any money or transferred any property to an attorney for services in connection with this case and that I will neither make any payment nor transfer any property for services in connection with this case until the filing fee is paid in full.

4.   I propose the following terms for the payment of the Filing Fee.*

$ _____   Check one ☐   With the filing of the petition, or
                                 ☐   On or before _____

$ _____   on or before _____

$ _____   on or before _____

$ _____   on or before _____

*   The number of installments proposed shall not exceed four (4), and the final installment shall be payable not later than 120 days after filing the petition. For cause shown, the court may extend the time of any installment, provided the last installment is paid not later than 180 days after filing the petition. Fed. R. Bankr. P. 1006(b)(2).

5.   I understand that if I fail to pay any installment when due my bankruptcy case may be dismissed and I may not receive a discharge of my debts.

_____   _____   _____   _____
Signature of Attorney   Date   Signature of Debtor   Date
                                                  (In a joint case, both spouses must sign.)

_____   _____   _____
Name of Attorney   Signature of Joint Debtor (if any)   Date

CERTIFICATION AND SIGNATURE OF NON-ATTORNEY BANKRUPTCY PETITION (See 11 U.S.C. § 110)

I certify that I am a bankruptcy petition preparer as defined in 11 U.S.C. § 110, that I prepared this document for compensation, and that I have provided the debtor with a copy of this document. I also certify that I will not accept money or any other property from the debtor before the filing fee is paid in full.

_____   _____
Printed or Typed Name of Bankruptcy Petition Preparer   Social Security No.

_____

_____

Address

Names and Social Security numbers of all other individuals who prepared or assisted in preparing this document:

If more than one person prepared this document, attach additional signed sheets conforming to the appropriate Official Form for each person.

x_____   _____
Signature of Bankruptcy Petition Preparer   Date

A bankruptcy petition preparer's failure to comply with the provisions of title 11 and the Federal Rules of Bankruptcy Procedure may result in fines or imprisonment or both. 11 U.S.C. § 110; 18 U.S.C. § 156.

UNITED STATES BANKRUPTCY COURT
_____ DISTRICT OF _____

In re _____,
             Debtor

Case No. _____

Chapter _____

ORDER APPROVING PAYMENT OF FILING FEE IN INSTALLMENTS

       IT IS ORDERED that the debtor(s) may pay the filing fee in installments on the terms proposed in the foregoing application.

       IT IS FURTHER ORDERED that until the filing fee is paid in full the debtor shall not pay any money for services in connection with this case, and the debtor shall not relinquish any property as payment for services in connection with this case.

BY THE COURT

Date: _____

_____
United States Bankruptcy Judge

168

UNITED STATES BANKRUPTCY COURT

_____**District of** _____

In re _____,   Case No. _____

           Debtor   (If known)

SUMMARY OF SCHEDULES

Indicate as to each schedule whether that schedule is attached and state the number of pages in each. Report the totals from Schedules A, B, D, E, F, I, and J in the boxes provided. Add the amounts from Schedules A and B to determine the total amount of the debtor's assets. Add the amounts from Schedules D, E, and F to determine the total amount of the debtor's liabilities.

			AMOUNTS SCHEDULED		
NAME OF SCHEDULE	**ATTACHED (YES/NO)**	**NO. OF SHEETS**	**ASSETS**	**LIABILITIES**	**OTHER**
A - Real Property			$		
B - Personal Property			$		
C - Property Claimed as Exempt					
D - Creditors Holding Secured Claims				$	
E - Creditors Holding Unsecured Priority Claims				$	
F - Creditors Holding Unsecured Nonpriority Claims				$	
G - Executory Contracts and Unexpired Leases					
H - Codebtors					
I - Current Income of Individual Debtor(s)					$
J - Current Expenditures of Individual Debtor(s)					$
Total Number of Sheets of ALL Schedules ➤					
Total Assets ➤			$		
Total Liabilities➤				$	$

form 4

In re _____, Case No. _____
Debtor   **(If known)**

SCHEDULE A - REAL PROPERTY

Except as directed below, list all real property in which the debtor has any legal, equitable, or future interest, including all property owned as a co-tenant , community property, or in which the debtor has a life estate. Include any property in which the debtor holds rights and powers exercisable for the debtor's own benefit. If the debtor is married, state whether husband, wife, or both own the property by placing an "H," "W," "J," or "C" in the column labeled "Husband, Wife, Joint, or Community." If the debtor holds no interest in real property, write "None" under "Description and Location of Property."

Do not include interests in executory contracts and unexpired leases on this schedule. List them in Schedule G - Executory Contracts and Unexpired Leases.

If an entity claims to have a lien or hold a secured interest in any property, state the amount of the secured claim. See Schedule D. If no entity claims to hold a secured interest in the property, write "None" in the column labeled "Amount of Secured Claim."

If the debtor is an individual or if a joint petition is filed, state the amount of any exemption claimed in the property only in Schedule C - Property Claimed as Exempt.

DESCRIPTION AND LOCATION OF PROPERTY	NATURE OF DEBTOR'S INTEREST IN PROPERTY	HUSBAND, WIFE, JOINT, OR COMMUNITY	CURRENT MARKET VALUE OF DEBTOR'S INTEREST IN PROPERTY, WITHOUT DEDUCTING ANY SECURED CLAIM OR EXEMPTION	AMOUNT OF SECURED CLAIM

Total▶

(Report also on Summary of Schedules.)

In re _____,
          Debtor

Case No. _____
          (If known)

SCHEDULE B - PERSONAL PROPERTY

    Except as directed below, list all personal property of the debtor of whatever kind. If the debtor has no property in one or more of the categories, place an "x" in the appropriate position in the column labeled "None." If additional space is needed in any category, attach a separate sheet properly identified with the case name, case number, and the number of the category. If the debtor is married, state whether husband, wife, or both own the property by placing an "H," "W," "J," or "C" in the column labeled "Husband, Wife, Joint, or Community." If the debtor is an individual or a joint petition is filed, state the amount of any exemptions claimed only in Schedule C - Property Claimed as Exempt.

    Do not list interests in executory contracts and unexpired leases on this schedule. List them in Schedule G - Executory Contracts and Unexpired Leases.

    If the property is being held for the debtor by someone else, state that person's name and address under "Description and Location of Property."

TYPE OF PROPERTY	N O N E	DESCRIPTION AND LOCATION OF PROPERTY	HUSBAND, WIFE, JOINT, OR COMMUNITY	CURRENT MARKET VALUE OF DEBTOR'S INTEREST IN PROPERTY, WITH- OUT DEDUCTING ANY SECURED CLAIM OR EXEMPTION
1. Cash on hand.				
2. Checking, savings or other financial accounts, certificates of deposit, or shares in banks, savings and loan, thrift, building and loan, and homestead associations, or credit unions, brokerage houses, or cooperatives.				
3. Security deposits with public utilities, telephone companies, landlords, and others.				
4. Household goods and furnishings, including audio, video, and computer equipment.				
5. Books; pictures and other art objects; antiques; stamp, coin, record, tape, compact disc, and other collections or collectibles.				
6. Wearing apparel.				
7. Furs and jewelry.				
8. Firearms and sports, photographic, and other hobby equipment.				
9. Interests in insurance policies. Name insurance company of each policy and itemize surrender or refund value of each.				
10. Annuities. Itemize and name each issuer.				

In re _____,   Case No. _____
　　　　　Debtor   **(If known)**

SCHEDULE B - PERSONAL PROPERTY
(Continuation Sheet)

TYPE OF PROPERTY	N O N E	DESCRIPTION AND LOCATION OF PROPERTY	HUSBAND, WIFE, JOINT, OR COMMUNITY	CURRENT MARKET VALUE OF DEBTOR'S INTEREST IN PROPERTY, WITHOUT DEDUCTING ANY SECURED CLAIM OR EXEMPTION
11. Interests in IRA, ERISA, Keogh, or other pension or profit sharing plans. Itemize.				
12. Stock and interests in incorporated and unincorporated businesses. Itemize.				
13. Interests in partnerships or joint ventures. Itemize.				
14. Government and corporate bonds and other negotiable and non-negotiable instruments.				
15. Accounts receivable.				
16. Alimony, maintenance, support, and property settlements to which the debtor is or may be entitled. Give particulars.				
17. Other liquidated debts owing debtor including tax refunds. Give particulars.				
18. Equitable or future interests, life estates, and rights or powers exercisable for the benefit of the debtor other than those listed in Schedule of Real Property.				
19. Contingent and noncontingent interests in estate of a decedent, death benefit plan, life insurance policy, or trust.				
20. Other contingent and unliquidated claims of every nature, including tax refunds, counterclaims of the debtor, and rights to setoff claims. Give estimated value of each.				
21. Patents, copyrights, and other intellectual property. Give particulars.				
22. Licenses, franchises, and other general intangibles. Give particulars.				

In re _____,   Case No. _____

Debtor   **(If known)**

SCHEDULE B -PERSONAL PROPERTY
(Continuation Sheet)

TYPE OF PROPERTY	NONE	DESCRIPTION AND LOCATION OF PROPERTY	HUSBAND, WIFE, JOINT, OR COMMUNITY	CURRENT MARKET VALUE OF DEBTOR'S INTEREST IN PROPERTY, WITH-OUT DEDUCTING ANY SECURED CLAIM OR EXEMPTION
23. Automobiles, trucks, trailers, and other vehicles and accessories.				
24. Boats, motors, and accessories.				
25. Aircraft and accessories.				
26. Office equipment, furnishings, and supplies.				
27. Machinery, fixtures, equipment, and supplies used in business.				
28. Inventory.				
29. Animals.				
30. Crops - growing or harvested. Give particulars.				
31. Farming equipment and implements.				
32. Farm supplies, chemicals, and feed.				
33. Other personal property of any kind not already listed. Itemize.				

_____continuation sheets attached   Total☐ $ _____

(Include amounts from any continuation sheets attached. Report total also on Summary of Schedules.)

173

In re _____,   Case No. _____
      Debtor   **(If known)**

SCHEDULE C - PROPERTY CLAIMED AS EXEMPT

Debtor elects the exemptions to which debtor is entitled under:

(Check one box)

☐   11 U.S.C. § 522(b)(1): Exemptions provided in 11 U.S.C. § 522(d). **Note: These exemptions are available only in certain states.**

☐   11 U.S.C. § 522(b)(2): Exemptions available under applicable nonbankruptcy federal laws, state or local law where the debtor's domicile has been located for the 180 days immediately preceding the filing of the petition, or for a longer portion of the 180-day period than in any other place, and the debtor's interest as a tenant by the entirety or joint tenant to the extent the interest is exempt from process under applicable nonbankruptcy law.

DESCRIPTION OF PROPERTY	SPECIFY LAW PROVIDING EACH EXEMPTION	VALUE OF CLAIMED EXEMPTION	CURRENT MARKET VALUE OF PROPERTY WITHOUT DEDUCTING EXEMPTION

In re _____,   Case No. _____
            Debtor   **(If known)**

SCHEDULE D - CREDITORS HOLDING SECURED CLAIMS

State the name, mailing address, including zip code, and account number, if any, of all entities holding claims secured by property of the debtor as of the date of filing of the petition. List creditors holding all types of secured interests such as judgment liens, garnishments, statutory liens, mortgages, deeds of trust, and other security interests. List creditors in alphabetical order to the extent practicable. If all secured creditors will not fit on this page, use the continuation sheet provided.

If any entity other than a spouse in a joint case may be jointly liable on a claim, place an "X" in the column labeled "Codebtor," include the entity on the appropriate schedule of creditors, and complete Schedule H - Codebtors. If a joint petition is filed, state whether husband, wife, both of them, or the marital community may be liable on each claim by placing an "H," "W," "J," or "C" in the column labeled "Husband, Wife, Joint, or Community."

If the claim is contingent, place an "X" in the column labeled "Contingent." If the claim is unliquidated, place an "X" in the column labeled "Unliquidated." If the claim is disputed, place an "X" in the column labeled "Disputed." (You may need to place an "X" in more than one of these three columns.)

Report the total of all claims listed on this schedule in the box labeled "Total" on the last sheet of the completed schedule. Report this total also on the Summary of Schedules.

☐ Check this box if debtor has no creditors holding secured claims to report on this Schedule D.

CREDITOR'S NAME AND MAILING ADDRESS INCLUDING ZIP CODE	CODEBTOR	HUSBAND, WIFE, JOINT, OR COMMUNITY	DATE CLAIM WAS INCURRED, NATURE OF LIEN, AND DESCRIPTION AND MARKET VALUE OF PROPERTY SUBJECT TO LIEN	CONTINGENT	UNLIQUIDATED	DISPUTED	AMOUNT OF CLAIM WITHOUT DEDUCTING VALUE OF COLLATERAL	UNSECURED PORTION, IF ANY
ACCOUNT NO. 			 VALUE $					
ACCOUNT NO. 			 VALUE $					
ACCOUNT NO. 			 VALUE $					
ACCOUNT NO. 			 VALUE $					

_____continuation sheets attached

Subtotal▶ $ _____
(Total of this page)

Total▶ $ _____
(Use only on last page)

(Report total also on Summary of Schedules)

In re _____, Case No. _____
Debtor   (If known)

SCHEDULE D - CREDITORS HOLDING SECURED CLAIMS
(Continuation Sheet)

CREDITOR'S NAME AND MAILING ADDRESS INCLUDING ZIP CODE	CODEBTOR	HUSBAND, WIFE, JOINT, OR COMMUNITY	DATE CLAIM WAS INCURRED, NATURE OF LIEN, AND DESCRIPTION AND MARKET VALUE OF PROPERTY SUBJECT TO LIEN	CONTINGENT	UNLIQUIDATED	DISPUTED	AMOUNT OF CLAIM WITHOUT DEDUCTING VALUE OF COLLATERAL	UNSECURED PORTION, IF ANY
ACCOUNT NO.								
			VALUE $					
ACCOUNT NO.								
			VALUE $					
ACCOUNT NO.								
			VALUE $					
ACCOUNT NO.								
			VALUE $					
ACCOUNT NO.								
			VALUE $					

Sheet no. ___ of ___ continuation sheets attached to Schedule of Creditors Holding Secured Claims Subtotal▶ $ _____
(Total of this page)
Total▶ $ _____
(Use only on last page)
(Report total also on Summary of Schedules)

176

In re _____ . Case No._____

Debtor (if known)

SCHEDULE E - CREDITORS HOLDING UNSECURED PRIORITY CLAIMS

A complete list of claims entitled to priority, listed separately by type of priority, is to be set forth on the sheets provided. Only holders of unsecured claims entitled to priority should be listed in this schedule. In the boxes provided on the attached sheets, state the name and mailing address, including zip code, and account number, if any, of all entities holding priority claims against the debtor or the property of the debtor, as of the date of the filing of the petition.

If any entity other than a spouse in a joint case may be jointly liable on a claim, place an "X" in the column labeled "Codebtor," include the entity on the appropriate schedule of creditors, and complete Schedule H-Codebtors. If a joint petition is filed, state whether husband, wife, both of them or the marital community may be liable on each claim by placing an "H,""W,""J," or "C" in the column labeled "Husband, Wife, Joint, or Community."

If the claim is contingent, place an "X" in the column labeled "Contingent." If the claim is unliquidated, place an "X" in the column labeled "Unliquidated." If the claim is disputed, place an "X" in the column labeled "Disputed." (You may need to place an "X" in more than one of these three columns.)

Report the total of claims listed on each sheet in the box labeled "Subtotal" on each sheet. Report the total of all claims listed on this Schedule E in the box labeled "Total" on the last sheet of the completed schedule. Repeat this total also on the Summary of Schedules.

☐ Check this box if debtor has no creditors holding unsecured priority claims to report on this Schedule E.

TYPES OF PRIORITY CLAIMS (Check the appropriate box(es) below if claims in that category are listed on the attached sheets)

☐ **Extensions of credit in an involuntary case**

Claims arising in the ordinary course of the debtor's business or financial affairs after the commencement of the case but before the earlier of the appointment of a trustee or the order for relief. 11 U.S.C. § 507(a)(2).

☐ **Wages, salaries, and commissions**

Wages, salaries, and commissions, including vacation, severance, and sick leave pay owing to employees and commissions owing to qualifying independent sales representatives up to $4,300* per person earned within 90 days immediately preceding the filing of the original petition, or the cessation of business, whichever occurred first, to the extent provided in 11 U.S.C. § 507(a)(3).

☐ **Contributions to employee benefit plans**

Money owed to employee benefit plans for services rendered within 180 days immediately preceding the filing of the original petition, or the cessation of business, whichever occurred first, to the extent provided in 11 U.S.C. § 507(a)(4).

☐ **Certain farmers and fishermen**

Claims of certain farmers and fishermen, up to $4,300* per farmer or fisherman, against the debtor, as provided in 11 U.S.C. § 507(a)(5).

☐ **Deposits by individuals**

Claims of individuals up to $1,950* for deposits for the purchase, lease, or rental of property or services for personal, family, or household use, that were not delivered or provided. 11 U.S.C. § 507(a)(6).

In re _____ ,   Case No._____

                        Debtor   (if known)

☐ **Alimony, Maintenance, or Support**

Claims of a spouse, former spouse, or child of the debtor for alimony, maintenance, or support, to the extent provided in 11 U.S.C. § 507(a)(7).

☐ **Taxes and Certain Other Debts Owed to Governmental Units**

Taxes, customs duties, and penalties owing to federal, state, and local governmental units as set forth in 11 U.S.C. § 507(a)(8).

☐ **Commitments to Maintain the Capital of an Insured Depository Institution**

Claims based on commitments to the FDIC, RTC, Director of the Office of Thrift Supervision, Comptroller of the Currency, or Board of Governors of the Federal Reserve System, or their predecessors or successors, to maintain the capital of an insured depository institution. 11 U.S.C. § 507 (a)(9).

* Amounts are subject to adjustment on April 1, 2004, and every three years thereafter with respect to cases commenced on or after the

date of adjustment.

_____ continuation sheets attached

In re _____, Case No. _____
                    Debtor   (If known)

SCHEDULE E - CREDITORS HOLDING UNSECURED PRIORITY CLAIMS
(Continuation Sheet)

_____
TYPE OF PRIORITY

CREDITOR'S NAME AND MAILING ADDRESS INCLUDING ZIP CODE	CODEBTOR	HUSBAND, WIFE, JOINT, OR COMMUNITY	DATE CLAIM WAS INCURRED AND CONSIDERATION FOR CLAIM	CONTINGENT	UNLIQUIDATED	DISPUTED	TOTAL AMOUNT OF CLAIM	AMOUNT ENTITLED TO PRIORITY
ACCOUNT NO.								
ACCOUNT NO.								
ACCOUNT NO.								
ACCOUNT NO.								
ACCOUNT NO.								

Sheet no. ___ of ___ sheets attached to Schedule of Creditors
Holding Priority Claims

Subtotal➤ $ _____
(Total of this page)
Total➤ $ _____
(Use only on last page of the completed Schedule E.)
(Report total also on Summary of Schedules)

In re _____ ,   Case No. _____
               Debtor   (If known)

SCHEDULE F- CREDITORS HOLDING UNSECURED NONPRIORITY CLAIMS

State the name, mailing address, including zip code, and account number, if any, of all entities holding unsecured claims without priority against the debtor or the property of the debtor, as of the date of filing of the petition. Do not include claims listed in Schedules D and E. If all creditors will not fit on this page, use the continuation sheet provided.

If any entity other than a spouse in a joint case may be jointly liable on a claim, place an "X" in the column labeled "Codebtor," include the entity on the appropriate schedule of creditors, and complete Schedule H - Codebtors. If a joint petition is filed, state whether husband, wife, both of them, or the marital community maybe liable on each claim by placing an "H," "W," "J," or "C" in the column labeled "Husband, Wife, Joint, or Community."

If the claim is contingent, place an "X" in the column labeled "Contingent." If the claim is unliquidated, place an "X" in the column labeled "Unliquidated." If the claim is disputed, place an "X" in the column labeled "Disputed." (You may need to place an "X" in more than one of these three columns.)

Report total of all claims listed on this schedule in the box labeled "Total" on the last sheet of the completed schedule. Report this total also on the Summary of Schedules.

☐ Check this box if debtor has no creditors holding unsecured claims to report on this Schedule F.

CREDITOR'S NAME AND MAILING ADDRESS INCLUDING ZIP CODE	CODEBTOR	HUSBAND, WIFE, JOINT, OR COMMUNITY	DATE CLAIM WAS INCURRED AND CONSIDERATION FOR CLAIM. IF CLAIM IS SUBJECT TO SETOFF, SO STATE.	CONTINGENT	UNLIQUIDATED	DISPUTED	AMOUNT OF CLAIM
ACCOUNT NO.							
ACCOUNT NO.							
ACCOUNT NO.							
ACCOUNT NO.							

_____continuation sheets attached   Subtotal➤ $

Total ➤ $
(Report also on Summary of Schedules)

In re _____, Case No. _____
                Debtor   (If known)

SCHEDULE F - CREDITORS HOLDING UNSECURED NONPRIORITY CLAIMS
(Continuation Sheet)

CREDITOR'S NAME AND MAILING ADDRESS INCLUDING ZIP CODE	CODEBTOR	HUSBAND, WIFE, JOINT, OR COMMUNITY	DATE CLAIM WAS INCURRED, AND CONSIDERATION FOR CLAIM. IF CLAIM IS SUBJECT TO SETOFF, SO STATE.	CONTINGENT	UNLIQUIDATED	DISPUTED	AMOUNT OF CLAIM
ACCOUNT NO.							
ACCOUNT NO.							
ACCOUNT NO.							
ACCOUNT NO.							
ACCOUNT NO.							

Sheet no. ___ of ___sheets attached to Schedule of
Creditors Holding Unsecured Nonpriority Claims

Subtotal ➤ $ _____
(Total of this page)

Total ➤ $ _____
(Use only on last page of the completed Schedule E.)
(Report total also on Summary of Schedules)

In re _____ ,   Case No._____
                Debtor   **(if known)**

SCHEDULE G - EXECUTORY CONTRACTS AND UNEXPIRED LEASES

Describe all executory contracts of any nature and all unexpired leases of real or personal property. Include any timeshare interests.

State nature of debtor's interest in contract, i.e., "Purchaser," "Agent," etc. State whether debtor is the lessor or lessee of a lease.

Provide the names and complete mailing addresses of all other parties to each lease or contract described.

NOTE: A party listed on this schedule will not receive notice of the filing of this case unless the party is also scheduled in the appropriate schedule of creditors.

☐   Check this box if debtor has no executory contracts or unexpired leases.

NAME AND MAILING ADDRESS, INCLUDING ZIP CODE, OF OTHER PARTIES TO LEASE OR CONTRACT.	DESCRIPTION OF CONTRACT OR LEASE AND NATURE OF DEBTOR'S INTEREST. STATE WHETHER LEASE IS FOR NONRESIDENTIAL REAL PROPERTY. STATE CONTRACT NUMBER OF ANY GOVERNMENT CONTRACT.

In re _____ ,   Case No. _____
                Debtor   **(if known)**

SCHEDULE H - CODEBTORS

     Provide the information requested concerning any person or entity, other than a spouse in a joint case, that is also liable on any debts listed by debtor in the schedules of creditors. Include all guarantors and co-signers. In community property states, a married debtor not filing a joint case should report the name and address of the nondebtor spouse on this schedule. Include all names used by the nondebtor spouse during the six years immediately preceding the commencement of this case.

☐ Check this box if debtor has no codebtors.

NAME AND ADDRESS OF CODEBTOR	NAME AND ADDRESS OF CREDITOR

In re _____ ,   Case No._____
                    Debtor   **(if known)**

SCHEDULE I - CURRENT INCOME OF INDIVIDUAL DEBTOR(S)

The column labeled "Spouse" must be completed in all cases filed by joint debtors and by a married debtor in a chapter 12 or 13 case whether or not a joint petition is filed, unless the spouses are separated and a joint petition is not filed.

Debtor's Marital Status:	DEPENDENTS OF DEBTOR AND SPOUSE		
	NAMES	AGE	RELATIONSHIP

Employment:	DEBTOR	SPOUSE
Occupation		
Name of Employer		
How long employed		
Address of Employer		

	DEBTOR	SPOUSE
Income: (Estimate of average monthly income)		
Current monthly gross wages, salary, and commissions (pro rate if not paid monthly.)	$_____	$_____
Estimated monthly overtime	$_____	$_____
SUBTOTAL	$_____	$_____
LESS PAYROLL DEDUCTIONS		
a. Payroll taxes and social security	$_____	$_____
b. Insurance	$_____	$_____
c. Union dues	$_____	$_____
d. Other (Specify: _____)	$_____	$_____
SUBTOTAL OF PAYROLL DEDUCTIONS	$_____	$_____
TOTAL NET MONTHLY TAKE HOME PAY	$_____	$_____
Regular income from operation of business or profession or farm (attach detailed statement)	$_____	$_____
Income from real property	$_____	$_____
Interest and dividends	$_____	$_____
Alimony, maintenance or support payments payable to the debtor for the debtor's use or that of dependents listed above.	$_____	$_____
Social security or other government assistance (Specify) _____	$_____	$_____
Pension or retirement income	$_____	$_____
Other monthly income	$_____	$_____
(Specify) _____	$_____	$_____
_____	$_____	$_____
TOTAL MONTHLY INCOME	$_____	$_____

TOTAL COMBINED MONTHLY INCOME $_____   (Report also on Summary of Schedules)

Describe any increase or decrease of more than 10% in any of the above categories anticipated to occur within the year following the filing of this document:

In re _____,   Case No._____
                  Debtor   **(if known)**

SCHEDULE J - CURRENT EXPENDITURES OF INDIVIDUAL DEBTOR(S)

Complete this schedule by estimating the average monthly expenses of the debtor and the debtor's family. Pro rate any payments made bi-weekly, quarterly, semi-annually, or annually to show monthly rate.

____   Check this box if a joint petition is filed and debtor's spouse maintains a separate household. Complete a separate schedule of expenditures labeled "Spouse."

Rent or home mortgage payment (include lot rented for mobile home)	$ _____
Are real estate taxes included? Yes _____ No _____	
Is property insurance included? Yes _____ No _____	
Utilities Electricity and heating fuel	$ _____
Water and sewer	$ _____
Telephone	$ _____
Other _____	$ _____
Home maintenance (repairs and upkeep)	$ _____
Food	$ _____
Clothing	$ _____
Laundry and dry cleaning	$ _____
Medical and dental expenses	$ _____
Transportation (not including car payments)	$ _____
Recreation, clubs and entertainment, newspapers, magazines, etc.	$ _____
Charitable contributions	$ _____
Insurance (not deducted from wages or included in home mortgage payments)	
Homeowner's or renter's	$ _____
Life	$ _____
Health	$ _____
Auto	$ _____
Other _____	$ _____
Taxes (not deducted from wages or included in home mortgage payments) (Specify) _____	$ _____
Installment payments: (In chapter 12 and 13 cases, do not list payments to be included in the plan)	
Auto	$ _____
Other _____	$ _____
Other _____	$ _____
Alimony, maintenance, and support paid to others	$ _____
Payments for support of additional dependents not living at your home	$ _____
Regular expenses from operation of business, profession, or farm (attach detailed statement)	$ _____
Other _____	$ _____
TOTAL MONTHLY EXPENSES (Report also on Summary of Schedules)	$ _____

[FOR CHAPTER 12 AND 13 DEBTORS ONLY]
Provide the information requested below, including whether plan payments are to be made bi-weekly, monthly, annually, or at some other regular interval.

A. Total projected monthly income	$ _____
B. Total projected monthly expenses	$ _____
C. Excess income (A minus B)	$ _____
D. Total amount to be paid into plan each _____	$ _____
(interval)	

form 14

In re _____ ,   Case No. _____
                    Debtor   (If known)

DECLARATION CONCERNING DEBTOR'S SCHEDULES

DECLARATION UNDER PENALTY OF PERJURY BY INDIVIDUAL DEBTOR

I declare under penalty of perjury that I have read the foregoing summary and schedules, consisting of _____
                                                                                      (Total shown on summary page plus 1.)
sheets, and that they are true and correct to the best of my knowledge, information, and belief.

Date _____   Signature: _____
                                                            Debtor

Date _____   Signature: _____
                                                     (Joint Debtor, if any)

                                          [If joint case, both spouses must sign.]

CERTIFICATION AND SIGNATURE OF NON-ATTORNEY BANKRUPTCY PETITION PREPARER (See 11 U.S.C. § 110)

I certify that I am a bankruptcy petition preparer as defined in 11 U.S.C. § 110, that I prepared this document for compensation, and that I have provided the debtor with a copy of this document.

_____   _____
Printed or Typed Name of Bankruptcy Petition Preparer   Social Security No.

_____

_____
Address

Names and Social Security numbers of all other individuals who prepared or assisted in preparing this document:

If more than one person prepared this document, attach additional signed sheets conforming to the appropriate Official Form for each person.

X _____   _____
Signature of Bankruptcy Petition Preparer   Date

A bankruptcy petition preparer's failure to comply with the provisions of title 11 and the Federal Rules of Bankruptcy Procedure may result in fines or imprisonment or both. 11 U.S.C. § 110; 18 U.S.C. § 156.

DECLARATION UNDER PENALTY OF PERJURY ON BEHALF OF A CORPORATION OR PARTNERSHIP

I, the _____ [the president or other officer or an authorized agent of the corporation or a member or an authorized agent of the partnership] of the _____ [corporation or partnership] named as debtor in this case, declare under penalty of perjury that I have read the foregoing summary and schedules, consisting of _____ sheets, and that they are true and correct to the best of my knowledge, information, and belief.   *(Total shown on summary page plus 1.)*

Date _____

                    Signature: _____

                              _____
                              [Print or type name of individual signing on behalf of debtor.]

[An individual signing on behalf of a partnership or corporation must indicate position or relationship to debtor.]

Penalty for making a false statement or concealing property: Fine of up to $500,000 or imprisonment for up to 5 years or both. 18 U.S.C. §§ 152 and 3571.

186

FORM 7. STATEMENT OF FINANCIAL AFFAIRS

UNITED STATES BANKRUPTCY COURT

_____ **DISTRICT OF** _____

In re: _____,   Case No. _____
            (Name)   (if known)
                        Debtor

STATEMENT OF FINANCIAL AFFAIRS

    This statement is to be completed by every debtor. Spouses filing a joint petition may file a single statement on which the information for both spouses is combined. If the case is filed under chapter 12 or chapter 13, a married debtor must furnish information for both spouses whether or not a joint petition is filed, unless the spouses are separated and a joint petition is not filed. An individual debtor engaged in business as a sole proprietor, partner, family farmer, or self-employed professional, should provide the information requested on this statement concerning all such activities as well as the individual's personal affairs.

    Questions 1 - 18 are to be completed by all debtors. Debtors that are or have been in business, as defined below, also must complete Questions 19 - 25. **If the answer to an applicable question is "None," mark the box labeled "None."** If additional space is needed for the answer to any question, use and attach a separate sheet properly identified with the case name, case number (if known), and the number of the question.

DEFINITIONS

    "In business." A debtor is "in business" for the purpose of this form if the debtor is a corporation or partnership. An individual debtor is "in business" for the purpose of this form if the debtor is or has been, within the six years immediately preceding the filing of this bankruptcy case, any of the following: an officer, director, managing executive, or owner of 5 percent or more of the voting or equity securities of a corporation; a partner, other than a limited partner, of a partnership; a sole proprietor or self-employed.

    "Insider." The term "insider" includes but is not limited to: relatives of the debtor; general partners of the debtor and their relatives; corporations of which the debtor is an officer, director, or person in control; officers, directors, and any owner of 5 percent or more of the voting or equity securities of a corporate debtor and their relatives; affiliates of the debtor and insiders of such affiliates; any managing agent of the debtor. 11 U.S.C. § 101.

_____

1. **Income from employment or operation of business**

None   State the gross amount of income the debtor has received from employment, trade, or profession, or from operation of
☐   the debtor's business from the beginning of this calendar year to the date this case was commenced. State also the gross
         amounts received during the **two years** immediately preceding this calendar year. (A debtor that maintains, or has
         maintained, financial records on the basis of a fiscal rather than a calendar year may report fiscal year income. Identify
         the beginning and ending dates of the debtor's fiscal year.) If a joint petition is filed, state income for each spouse
         separately. (Married debtors filing under chapter 12 or chapter 13 must state income of both spouses whether or not a
         joint petition is filed, unless the spouses are separated and a joint petition is not filed.)

                AMOUNT   SOURCE (if more than one)

2. Income other than from employment or operation of business

None

☐

State the amount of income received by the debtor other than from employment, trade, profession, or operation of the debtor's business during the **two years** immediately preceding the commencement of this case. Give particulars. If a joint petition is filed, state income for each spouse separately. (Married debtors filing under chapter 12 or chapter 13 must state income for each spouse whether or not a joint petition is filed, unless the spouses are separated and a joint petition is not filed.)

AMOUNT	SOURCE

3. Payments to creditors

None

☐

a. List all payments on loans, installment purchases of goods or services, and other debts, aggregating more than $600 to any creditor, made within **90 days** immediately preceding the commencement of this case. (Married debtors filing under chapter 12 or chapter 13 must include payments by either or both spouses whether or not a joint petition is filed, unless the spouses are separated and a joint petition is not filed.)

NAME AND ADDRESS OF CREDITOR	DATES OF PAYMENTS	AMOUNT PAID	AMOUNT STILL OWING

None

☐

b. List all payments made within **one year** immediately preceding the commencement of this case to or for the benefit of creditors who are or were insiders. (Married debtors filing under chapter 12 or chapter 13 must include payments by either or both spouses whether or not a joint petition is filed, unless the spouses are separated and a joint petition is not filed.)

NAME AND ADDRESS OF CREDITOR AND RELATIONSHIP TO DEBTOR	DATE OF PAYMENT	AMOUNT PAID	AMOUNT STILL OWING

4. Suits and administrative proceedings, executions, garnishments and attachments

None

☐

a. List all suits and administrative proceedings to which the debtor is or was a party within **one year** immediately preceding the filing of this bankruptcy case. (Married debtors filing under chapter 12 or chapter 13 must include information concerning either or both spouses whether or not a joint petition is filed, unless the spouses are separated and a joint petition is not filed.)

CAPTION OF SUIT AND CASE NUMBER	NATURE OF PROCEEDING	COURT OR AGENCY AND LOCATION	STATUS OR DISPOSITION

None ☐   b.   Describe all property that has been attached, garnished or seized under any legal or equitable process within **one year** immediately preceding the commencement of this case. (Married debtors filing under chapter 12 or chapter 13 must include information concerning property of either or both spouses whether or not a joint petition is filed, unless the spouses are separated and a joint petition is not filed.)

NAME AND ADDRESS OF PERSON FOR WHOSE BENEFIT PROPERTY WAS SEIZED	DATE OF SEIZURE	DESCRIPTION AND VALUE OF PROPERTY

---

5.   Repossessions, foreclosures and returns

None ☐   List all property that has been repossessed by a creditor, sold at a foreclosure sale, transferred through a deed in lieu of foreclosure or returned to the seller, within **one year** immediately preceding the commencement of this case. (Married debtors filing under chapter 12 or chapter 13 must include information concerning property of either or both spouses whether or not a joint petition is filed, unless the spouses are separated and a joint petition is not filed.)

NAME AND ADDRESS OF CREDITOR OR SELLER	DATE OF REPOSSESSION, FORECLOSURE SALE, TRANSFER OR RETURN	DESCRIPTION AND VALUE OF PROPERTY

---

6.   Assignments and receiverships

None ☐   a.   Describe any assignment of property for the benefit of creditors made within **120 days** immediately preceding the commencement of this case. (Married debtors filing under chapter 12 or chapter 13 must include any assignment by either or both spouses whether or not a joint petition is filed, unless the spouses are separated and a joint petition is not filed.)

NAME AND ADDRESS OF ASSIGNEE	DATE OF ASSIGNMENT	TERMS OF ASSIGNMENT OR SETTLEMENT

None ☐   b.   List all property which has been in the hands of a custodian, receiver, or court-appointed official within **one year** immediately preceding the commencement of this case. (Married debtors filing under chapter 12 or chapter 13 must include information concerning property of either or both spouses whether or not a joint petition is filed, unless the spouses are separated and a joint petition is not filed.)

NAME AND ADDRESS OF CUSTODIAN	NAME AND LOCATION OF COURT CASE TITLE & NUMBER	DATE OF ORDER	DESCRIPTION AND VALUE OF PROPERTY

7. Gifts

None
☐

List all gifts or charitable contributions made within **one year** immediately preceding the commencement of this case except ordinary and usual gifts to family members aggregating less than $200 in value per individual family member and charitable contributions aggregating less than $100 per recipient. (Married debtors filing under chapter 12 or chapter 13 must include gifts or contributions by either or both spouses whether or not a joint petition is filed, unless the spouses are separated and a joint petition is not filed.)

NAME AND ADDRESS OF PERSON OR ORGANIZATION	RELATIONSHIP TO DEBTOR, IF ANY	DATE OF GIFT	DESCRIPTION AND VALUE OF GIFT

8. Losses

None
☐

List all losses from fire, theft, other casualty or gambling within **one year** immediately preceding the commencement of this case **or since the commencement of this case**. (Married debtors filing under chapter 12 or chapter 13 must include losses by either or both spouses whether or not a joint petition is filed, unless the spouses are separated and a joint petition is not filed.)

DESCRIPTION AND VALUE OF PROPERTY	DESCRIPTION OF CIRCUMSTANCES AND, IF LOSS WAS COVERED IN WHOLE OR IN PART BY INSURANCE, GIVE PARTICULARS	DATE OF LOSS

9. Payments related to debt counseling or bankruptcy

None
☐

List all payments made or property transferred by or on behalf of the debtor to any persons, including attorneys, for consultation concerning debt consolidation, relief under the bankruptcy law or preparation of a petition in bankruptcy within **one year** immediately preceding the commencement of this case.

NAME AND ADDRESS OF PAYEE	DATE OF PAYMENT, NAME OF PAYOR IF OTHER THAN DEBTOR	AMOUNT OF MONEY OR DESCRIPTION AND VALUE OF PROPERTY

10. Other transfers

None
☐

List all other property, other than property transferred in the ordinary course of the business or financial affairs of the debtor, transferred either absolutely or as security within **one year** immediately preceding the commencement of this case. (Married debtors filing under chapter 12 or chapter 13 must include transfers by either or both spouses whether or not a joint petition is filed, unless the spouses are separated and a joint petition is not filed.)

NAME AND ADDRESS OF TRANSFEREE, RELATIONSHIP TO DEBTOR	DATE	DESCRIBE PROPERTY TRANSFERRED AND VALUE RECEIVED

11. Closed financial accounts

None ☐ List all financial accounts and instruments held in the name of the debtor or for the benefit of the debtor which were closed, sold, or otherwise transferred within **one year** immediately preceding the commencement of this case. Include checking, savings, or other financial accounts, certificates of deposit, or other instruments; shares and share accounts held in banks, credit unions, pension funds, cooperatives, associations, brokerage houses and other financial institutions. (Married debtors filing under chapter 12 or chapter 13 must include information concerning accounts or instruments held by or for either or both spouses whether or not a joint petition is filed, unless the spouses are separated and a joint petition is not filed.)

NAME AND ADDRESS OF INSTITUTION	TYPE AND NUMBER OF ACCOUNT AND AMOUNT OF FINAL BALANCE	AMOUNT AND DATE OF SALE OR CLOSING

12. Safe deposit boxes

None ☐ List each safe deposit or other box or depository in which the debtor has or had securities, cash, or other valuables within **one year** immediately preceding the commencement of this case. (Married debtors filing under chapter 12 or chapter 13 must include boxes or depositories of either or both spouses whether or not a joint petition is filed, unless the spouses are separated and a joint petition is not filed.)

NAME AND ADDRESS OF BANK OR OTHER DEPOSITORY	NAMES AND ADDRESSES OF THOSE WITH ACCESS TO BOX OR DEPOSITORY	DESCRIPTION OF CONTENTS	DATE OF TRANSFER OR SURRENDER, IF ANY

13. Setoffs

None ☐ List all setoffs made by any creditor, including a bank, against a debt or deposit of the debtor within **90 days** preceding the commencement of this case. (Married debtors filing under chapter 12 or chapter 13 must include information concerning either or both spouses whether or not a joint petition is filed, unless the spouses are separated and a joint petition is not filed.)

NAME AND ADDRESS OF CREDITOR	DATE OF SETOFF	AMOUNT OF SETOFF

14. Property held for another person

None ☐ List all property owned by another person that the debtor holds or controls.

NAME AND ADDRESS OF OWNER	DESCRIPTION AND VALUE OF PROPERTY	LOCATION OF PROPERTY

15. Prior address of debtor

None
☐

If the debtor has moved within the **two years** immediately preceding the commencement of this case, list all premises which the debtor occupied during that period and vacated prior to the commencement of this case. If a joint petition is filed, report also any separate address of either spouse.

ADDRESS   NAME USED   DATES OF OCCUPANCY

16. Spouses and Former Spouses

None
☐

If the debtor resides or resided in a community property state, commonwealth, or territory (including Alaska, Arizona, California, Idaho, Louisiana, Nevada, New Mexico, Puerto Rico, Texas, Washington, or Wisconsin) within the **six-year period** immediately preceding the commencement of the case, identify the name of the debtor's spouse and of any former spouse who resides or resided with the debtor in the community property state.

NAME

17. Environmental Information.

For the purpose of this question, the following definitions apply:

"Environmental Law" means any federal, state, or local statute or regulation regulating pollution, contamination, releases of hazardous or toxic substances, wastes or material into the air, land, soil, surface water, groundwater, or other medium, including, but not limited to, statutes or regulations regulating the cleanup of these substances, wastes, or material.

"Site" means any location, facility, or property as defined under any Environmental Law, whether or not presently or formerly owned or operated by the debtor, including, but not limited to, disposal sites.

"Hazardous Material" means anything defined as a hazardous waste, hazardous substance, toxic substance, hazardous material, pollutant, or contaminant or similar term under an Environmental Law

None
☐

a. List the name and address of every site for which the debtor has received notice in writing by a governmental unit that it may be liable or potentially liable under or in violation of an Environmental Law. Indicate the governmental unit, the date of the notice, and, if known, the Environmental Law:

SITE NAME   NAME AND ADDRESS   DATE OF   ENVIRONMENTAL
AND ADDRESS   OF GOVERNMENTAL UNIT   NOTICE   LAW

None
☐

b. List the name and address of every site for which the debtor provided notice to a governmental unit of a release of Hazardous Material. Indicate the governmental unit to which the notice was sent and the date of the notice.

SITE NAME   NAME AND ADDRESS   DATE OF   ENVIRONMENTAL
AND ADDRESS   OF GOVERNMENTAL UNIT   NOTICE   LAW

None
c. List all judicial or administrative proceedings, including settlements or orders, under any Environmental Law with

□ respect to which the debtor is or was a party. Indicate the name and address of the governmental unit that is or was a party to the proceeding, and the docket number.

NAME AND ADDRESS OF GOVERNMENTAL UNIT	DOCKET NUMBER	STATUS OR DISPOSITION

---

18 . Nature, location and name of business

None
□

a.   If the debtor is an individual, list the names, addresses, taxpayer identification numbers, nature of the businesses, and beginning and ending dates of all businesses in which the debtor was an officer, director, partner, or managing executive of a corporation, partnership, sole proprietorship, or was a self-employed professional within the **six years** immediately preceding the commencement of this case, or in which the debtor owned 5 percent or more of the voting or equity securities within the **six years** immediately preceding the commencement of this case.

If the debtor is a partnership, list the names, addresses, taxpayer identification numbers, nature of the businesses, and beginning and ending dates of all businesses in which the debtor was a partner or owned 5 percent or more of the voting or equity securities, within the **six years** immediately preceding the commencement of this case.

If the debtor is a corporation, list the names, addresses, taxpayer identification numbers, nature of the businesses, and beginning and ending dates of all businesses in which the debtor was a partner or owned 5 percent or more of the voting or equity securities within the **six years** immediately preceding the commencement of this case.

NAME	TAXPAYER I.D. NUMBER	ADDRESS	NATURE OF BUSINESS	BEGINNING AND ENDING DATES

None
□

b.   Identify any business listed in response to subdivision a., above, that is "single asset real estate" as defined in 11 U.S.C. § 101.

NAME	ADDRESS

The following questions are to be completed by every debtor that is a corporation or partnership and by any individual debtor who is or has been, within the **six years** immediately preceding the commencement of this case, any of the following: an officer, director, managing executive, or owner of more than 5 percent of the voting or equity securities of a corporation; a partner, other than a limited partner, of a partnership; a sole proprietor or otherwise self-employed.

*(An individual or joint debtor should complete this portion of the statement **only** if the debtor is or has been in business, as defined above, within the six years immediately preceding the commencement of this case. A debtor who has not been in business within those six years should go directly to the signature page.)*

19. Books, records and financial statements

None ☐

a. List all bookkeepers and accountants who within the **two years** immediately preceding the filing of this bankruptcy case kept or supervised the keeping of books of account and records of the debtor.

NAME AND ADDRESS	DATES SERVICES RENDERED

None ☐

b. List all firms or individuals who within the **two years** immediately preceding the filing of this bankruptcy case have audited the books of account and records, or prepared a financial statement of the debtor.

NAME	ADDRESS	DATES SERVICES RENDERED

None ☐

c. List all firms or individuals who at the time of the commencement of this case were in possession of the books of account and records of the debtor. If any of the books of account and records are not available, explain.

NAME	ADDRESS

None ☐

d. List all financial institutions, creditors and other parties, including mercantile and trade agencies, to whom a financial statement was issued within the **two years** immediately preceding the commencement of this case by the debtor.

NAME AND ADDRESS	DATE ISSUED

20. Inventories

None ☐

a. List the dates of the last two inventories taken of your property, the name of the person who supervised the taking of each inventory, and the dollar amount and basis of each inventory.

DATE OF INVENTORY	INVENTORY SUPERVISOR	DOLLAR AMOUNT OF INVENTORY (Specify cost, market or other basis)

None ☐

b. List the name and address of the person having possession of the records of each of the two inventories reported in a., above.

DATE OF INVENTORY	NAME AND ADDRESSES OF CUSTODIAN OF INVENTORY RECORDS

21 . Current Partners, Officers, Directors and Shareholders

None ☐

   a.   If the debtor is a partnership, list the nature and percentage of partnership interest of each member of the partnership.

NAME AND ADDRESS	NATURE OF INTEREST	PERCENTAGE OF INTEREST

None ☐

   b.   If the debtor is a corporation, list all officers and directors of the corporation, and each stockholder who directly or indirectly owns, controls, or holds 5 percent or more of the voting or equity securities of the corporation.

NAME AND ADDRESS	TITLE	NATURE AND PERCENTAGE OF STOCK OWNERSHIP

22 . Former partners, officers, directors and shareholders

None ☐

   a.   If the debtor is a partnership, list each member who withdrew from the partnership within **one year** immediately preceding the commencement of this case.

NAME	ADDRESS	DATE OF WITHDRAWAL

None ☐

   b.   If the debtor is a corporation, list all officers, or directors whose relationship with the corporation terminated within **one year** immediately preceding the commencement of this case.

NAME AND ADDRESS	TITLE	DATE OF TERMINATION

23 . Withdrawals from a partnership or distributions by a corporation

None ☐

If the debtor is a partnership or corporation, list all withdrawals or distributions credited or given to an insider, including compensation in any form, bonuses, loans, stock redemptions, options exercised and any other perquisite during **one year** immediately preceding the commencement of this case.

NAME & ADDRESS OF RECIPIENT, RELATIONSHIP TO DEBTOR	DATE AND PURPOSE OF WITHDRAWAL	AMOUNT OF MONEY OR DESCRIPTION AND VALUE OF PROPERTY

24. Tax Consolidation Group.

None
☐

If the debtor is a corporation, list the name and federal taxpayer identification number of the parent corporation of any consolidated group for tax purposes of which the debtor has been a member at any time within the **six-year period** immediately preceding the commencement of the case.

NAME OF PARENT CORPORATION   TAXPAYER IDENTIFICATION NUMBER

25. Pension Funds.

None
☐

If the debtor is not an individual, list the name and federal taxpayer identification number of any pension fund to which the debtor, as an employer, has been responsible for contributing at any time within the **six-year period** immediately preceding the commencement of the case.

NAME OF PENSION FUND   TAXPAYER IDENTIFICATION NUMBER

* * * * * *

[If completed by an individual or individual and spouse]

I declare under penalty of perjury that I have read the answers contained in the foregoing statement of financial affairs and any attachments thereto and that they are true and correct.

Date _____ Signature _____
of Debtor

Date _____ Signature _____
of Joint Debtor
(if any)

[If completed on behalf of a partnership or corporation]

I, declare under penalty of perjury that I have read the answers contained in the foregoing statement of financial affairs and any attachments thereto and that they are true and correct to the best of my knowledge, information and belief.

Date _____ Signature _____

_____
Print Name and Title

[An individual signing on behalf of a partnership or corporation must indicate position or relationship to debtor.]

_____ continuation sheets attached

Penalty for making a false statement: Fine of up to $500,000 or imprisonment for up to 5 years, or both. 18 U.S.C. § 152 and 3571

CERTIFICATION AND SIGNATURE OF NON-ATTORNEY BANKRUPTCY PETITION PREPARER (See 11 U.S.C. § 110)

I certify that I am a bankruptcy petition preparer as defined in 11 U.S.C. § 110, that I prepared this document for compensation, and that I have provided the debtor with a copy of this document.

_____   _____
Printed or Typed Name of Bankruptcy Petition Preparer   Social Security No.

_____

_____
Address

Names and Social Security numbers of all other individuals who prepared or assisted in preparing this document:

If more than one person prepared this document, attach additional signed sheets conforming to the appropriate Official Form for each person.

X _____   _____
Signature of Bankruptcy Petition Preparer   Date

A bankruptcy petition preparer's failure to comply with the provisions of title 11 and the Federal Rules of Bankruptcy Procedure may result in fines or imprisonment or both. 18 U.S.C. § 156.

⬤ ⬤

UNITED STATES BANKRUPTCY COURT
_____ DISTRICT OF _____

In re _____,
         Debtor

                                    Case No. _____

                                    Chapter _____

CHAPTER 7 INDIVIDUAL DEBTOR'S STATEMENT OF INTENTION

1. I have filed a schedule of assets and liabilities which includes consumer debts secured by property of the estate.

2. I intend to do the following with respect to the property of the estate which secures those consumer debts:

     a. *Property to Be Surrendered.*

Description of Property   **Creditor's name**

     b. *Property to Be Retained*   *[Check any applicable statement.]*

Description of Property	Creditor's Name	Property is claimed as exempt	Property will be redeemed pursuant to 11 U.S.C. § 722	Debt will be reaffirmed pursuant to 11 U.S.C. § 524(c)

Date: _____

                                      _____
                                           Signature of Debtor

----

CERTIFICATION OF NON-ATTORNEY BANKRUPTCY PETITION PREPARER (See 11 U.S.C. § 110)

   I certify that I am a bankruptcy petition preparer as defined in 11 U.S.C. § 110, that I prepared this document for compensation, and that I have provided the debtor with a copy of this document.

_____   _____
Printed or Typed Name of Bankruptcy Petition Preparer   Social Security No.

_____

_____
Address

Names and Social Security Numbers of all other individuals who prepared or assisted in preparing this document.

If more than one person prepared this document, attach additional signed sheets conforming to the appropriate Official Form for each person.

X_____   _____
Signature of Bankruptcy Petition Preparer   Date

A bankruptcy petition preparer's failure to comply with the provisions of title 11 and the Federal Rules of Bankruptcy Procedure may result in fines or imprisonment or both. 11 U.S.C. § 110; 18 U.S.C. § 156.

UNITED STATES BANKRUPTCY COURT
_____ DISTRICT OF _____

In re _____   Case No. _____
                Debtor   (if known)

CHAPTER 13 PLAN

The debtor shall pay to the trustee out of the debtor's future earnings or other income the sum of $_____ (weekly) (semi-monthly) (monthly). From the funds received the trustee shall make distribution as follows:

1. Expenses of administration and debts entitled to priority under 11 U.S.C. Section 507.

2. Payments to secured creditors whose claims are duly filed and allowed as follows:

3. From the balance remaining after the above payments, dividends to unsecured creditors whose claims are duly filed and allowed as follows:

4. Except as provided in this plan or in the order confirming this plan, upon confirmation of this plan, all property of the estate shall vest in the debtor free and clear of any claim or interest of any creditor provided for by this plan pursuant to 11 U.S.C. Section 1327.

5. [   ] See attached addendum for additional terms.

Dated: _____   _____
                                            Petitioner

                             _____
                                            Petitioner

```
                          )
                          )
                          )
                          )
        vs.               )      Case No. _____
                          )
                          )
                          )
                          )
```

SUGGESTION OF BANKRUPTCY

The Defendant(s), _____
hereby notifies this Court that said defendant(s) filed a Petition for Bankruptcy, in the
United States District Court on _____, a copy of said
petition is attached hereto.

Dated: _____   Signed: _____

                                          Defendant

                                         _____

                                          Defendant

CERTIFICATE OF SERVICE

I hereby certify that a copy of the foregoing was sent by first class, U.S. Mail on
_____, to the following parties:

_____

UNITED STATES BANKRUPTCY COURT
_____ DISTRICT OF _____

In re _____   Case No. _____
                Debtor   (if known)

PROOF OF SERVICE BY MAIL

I, _____ {name}, declare that:

I am over the age of 18 years and am not a party to the within bankruptcy.

I reside, or am employed, in the County of _____ {name of county}, _____ {state}.

My residence/business address is _____

_____.

On _____, 20___, I served the within _____

_____ {title of document(s) served} by placing a true and correct copy of it (them) in a sealed envelope with first-class postage fully prepaid, in the United States mail at _____ {post office location}, addressed as follows:

I declare under penalty of perjury that the foregoing is true and correct. Executed on _____, 20___, at _____ {city}, _____ {state}.

_____
Signature

UNITED STATES BANKRUPTCY COURT
_____ DISTRICT OF _____

In re _____   Case No. _____
       Debtor   (if known)

AMENDMENT COVER SHEET

The Debtor hereby files the attached amendment documents, consisting of:

         [   ] Voluntary Petition

         [   ] Summary of Schedules

         [   ] Schedule(s) _____

         [   ] Statement of Financial Affairs

         [   ] Chapter 7 Individual Debtor's Statement of Intention

         [   ] Chapter 13 Plan

         [   ] Other _____

UNSWORN DECLARATION UNDER PENALTY OF PERJURY

I, _____, and I, _____, declare under penalty of perjury that the information set forth above, and contained in the attached amendment documents, consisting of ___ pages, is true and correct to the best of my (our) information and belief.

Dated: _____   _____
                                         Debtor

                                         _____
                                         Debtor's Spouse

UNITED STATES BANKRUPTCY COURT

_____ DISTRICT OF _____

In re _____   Case No. _____
      Debtor   (if known)

MOTION TO CONVERT TO CHAPTER 7

The Debtor, having originally filed this action pursuant to Chapter 13 of the U.S. Bankruptcy Code, hereby moves this court to convert this action to a proceeding pursuant to Chapter 7 of the U.S. Bankruptcy Code. In furtherance of this motion the Debtor has attached a Chapter 7 Individual Debtor's Statement of Intention.

Dated: _____   _____
                              Petitioner

_____
Petitioner

ORDER

IN CONSIDERATION of the foregoing motion of the Debtor,

IT IS HEREBY ORDERED, that this action is converted to a proceeding pursuant to Chapter 7 of the U.S. Bankruptcy Code.

Dated: _____   _____
                              Judge

APPENDIX E
LETTERS

This appendix contains sample letters to creditors. Use them as a guide to writing letters to your own creditors.

NOTE: *Do not forget to sign and date any letter you send to a creditor.*

NOTE: *It is a good idea to send these letters by certified, return-receipt mail. This will cost you a couple of dollars per letter, but you will later be able to prove the creditor received it if needed.*

TABLE OF LETTERS

Dear Sir or Madam:

    YOU ARE HEREBY ADVISED that on _____,
I filed a voluntary petition with the U.S. Bankruptcy Code, you may not:

    -Take any action to evict me from my residence.

    -Discontinue any service or benefit being provided to me.

    -Take any action against me or my property, or repossess any of my property.

    Any violation of these prohibitions may constitute contempt of court and be punished accordingly.

                       Sincerely,

Dear Sir or Madam:

    My current financial situation may require me to file for bankruptcy protection. In order to avoid this, I am requesting that my payments on your account be restructured. This will allow me to pay you the full amount you are owed.

    My net monthly income is $ _____. After paying essential expenses, such as housing, utilities, food, clothing, transportation for work, and medical expenses, I am left with a monthly disposable income of $ _____. Out of this balance I am able to pay my creditors as follows

CREDITOR	OLD AMOUNT	REVISED AMOUNT

    This schedule represents an equal pro-rata reduction for each unsecured creditor. Please let me know if this new arrangement is acceptable. Unless I hear from you before the next payment is due, I will assume this proposal is acceptable, and will make my next payment according to the revised amount.

    Thank you for your attention to this matter.

                Sincerely,

INDEX